The C

A Photographic Album

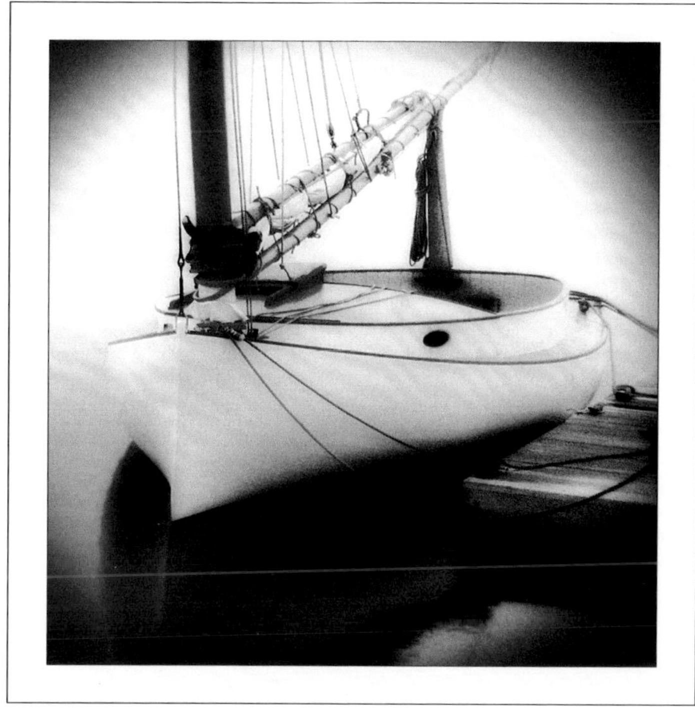

Images From the Collection
of
Mystic Seaport ~ The Museum of America and the Sea

Markham Starr

Fowler Road Press
49 Fowler Road
North Stonington, Ct 06359
Tel: 860.535.4413

ISBN-10: 0-9821685-1-9
ISBN-13: 978-0-9821685-1-6

First Edition Published: July - 2009
Book Design by Fowler Road Press

Frontispiece: *The Breck Marshall* by Markham Starr

Printed in China

The Catboat: A Brief Introduction

The Cape Cod cat is likely the model most people picture when they hear the word "catboat." They seem almost as New England as clam chowder itself. Their wide beams, plumb stems, massive rudders and stout masts in the eyes of the boat make them immediately recognizable to both sailors and non-sailors alike. Ironically, according to Howard Chapelle[1], the people of Cape Cod were late in their adaptation of this type of watercraft to their own use. The exact origin of the catboat along the northeast coast of the United States in the mid 1800's remains open to speculation. As with many other watercraft designs, it may simply have been the next step in the evolution of both hull forms and sailing rigs already in local use. The earliest examples of these vessels were found sailing in New York waters. As the type began to spread north and eastward into New England, changes were made to accommodate not only the different conditions encountered along these open coastlines, but also the different fisheries in which they would be employed. Having reached the mouth of Narragansett Bay, both Newport and Bristol Rhode Island became design centers for this new form, spreading their influence to both Martha's Vineyard and eventually Cape Cod itself.

While often used as a racing and pleasure craft in New York waters, the catboat took on the challenges of a working watercraft in its northern reaches. Because of this, boats such as the working cats built by the celebrated Crosby family in Oysterville were necessarily different. Deeper freeboards, higher bow profiles and reduced sail plans produced a craft that could handle the problematic waters along the south shore of the cape. They became stable work platforms from which to fish, thoroughly at home in the shoal areas between Cape Cod and Nantucket, whose strong currents and stiff breezes had to be considered. Designed as such, these vessels were safe and able craft. As is often the case, these vessels eventually began to garner the attention of local yachtsmen who sought to commandeer their desirable properties for their own use.

The requirements of the catboat for the local fishermen were, however, different from those of the general sailor. In light airs, the working cat's rigs were deemed too small, and as these images show, where changed to suit new criteria. Masts were lengthened and booms began reaching past the point where reefs could be tucked safely from the deck. Bowsprits were added with headsails to either improve handling or increase speed. With these extreme rigs and hulls came the catboat's new reputation as a dangerous craft, especially as accidents increased. William Alden, in his article *The Flying Proa*[2], had this to say about them: "The catboat swarms all over our harbors, rivers, and small lakes, and annually drowns a frightful aggregate of men, women, and boys." He goes on to fully list all of the dangerous behavioral characteristics of the type and indicates that he would be happy to see them disappear from the waterfront scene altogether.

With the passage of time, however, the catboat began to fade from New England's coastlines. Marine engines became more efficient, reliable and cost effective. Powered watercraft began to displace all forms of working vessels once driven by the wind. New hull forms and sailing rigs replaced those of the catboat as yachtsmen searched for more speed under sail. This commonplace design seemed doomed to fade into memory. The form did not, however, disappear altogether. Recreational forms of the type persist in boats such as the Marshall Cat or the Beetle Cat. The traditionally built wooden Beetle Cat, which first appeared in 1921, has done much to keep this American form alive, and is still a common sight today in the countless harbors and bays of our coastline. While fiberglass may have replaced wooden construction in larger boats, the catboat has reemerged in the form of day-sailors and small cruisers, with rigs of safe proportions once again. These images help remind us of the long tradition from which our modern counterparts sprung.

The Photographs

The images within this volume come from the extensive photographic collections of Mystic Seaport. With over 1.3 million images, the Museum houses one of the largest maritime collections in North America. The collection dates from the mid 1800's to present day, and the photographs within this volume run the gamut of photographic processes then available, from glass plate negatives to modern roll film. Some of these photographs are reproduced from nitrate negatives (a very unstable material,) original silver prints, and even magic lantern slides, an early form of photographs made for projection. Most of the catboats pictured here are from images taken in the late 1800's into the middle of the last century, and depict the catboat as pleasure craft. Not surprisingly, there are few images in the Museum's collection of working catboats. Common to the waterfront and of lower pedigree than the pleasure craft represented here, working catboats were less often the subject of waterfront photographers.

Most of the photographs within this book are old enough to have required some digital restoration. I have tried to remain faithful to the intent of the original photographer in their repair. The images were chosen with a variety in style, content, and vessel type to best represent the catboats found within the Museum's collection. The information below each photograph comes from curatorial records, and reflects what, if anything, is known about the image in particular. I hope you enjoy this glimpse into the wonderful past of the catboat.

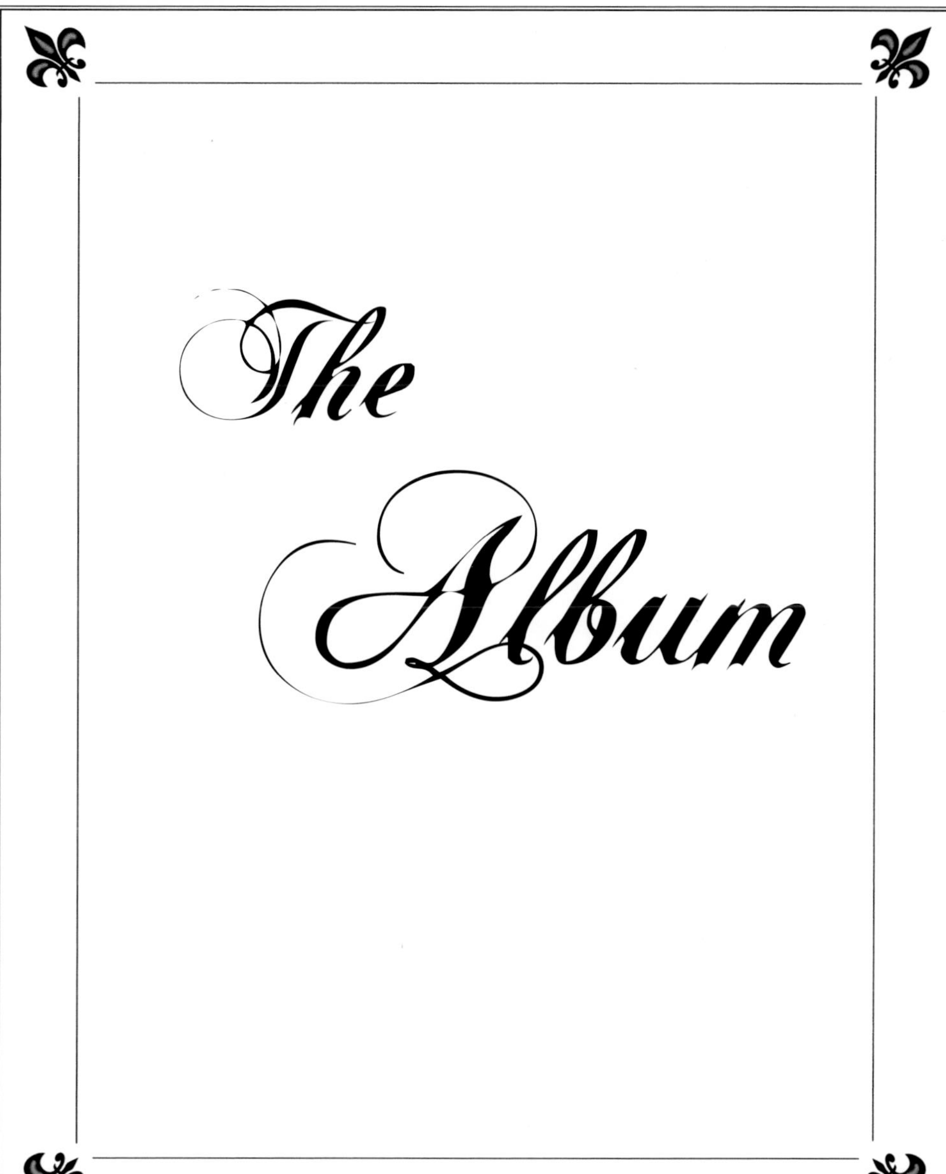
The Album

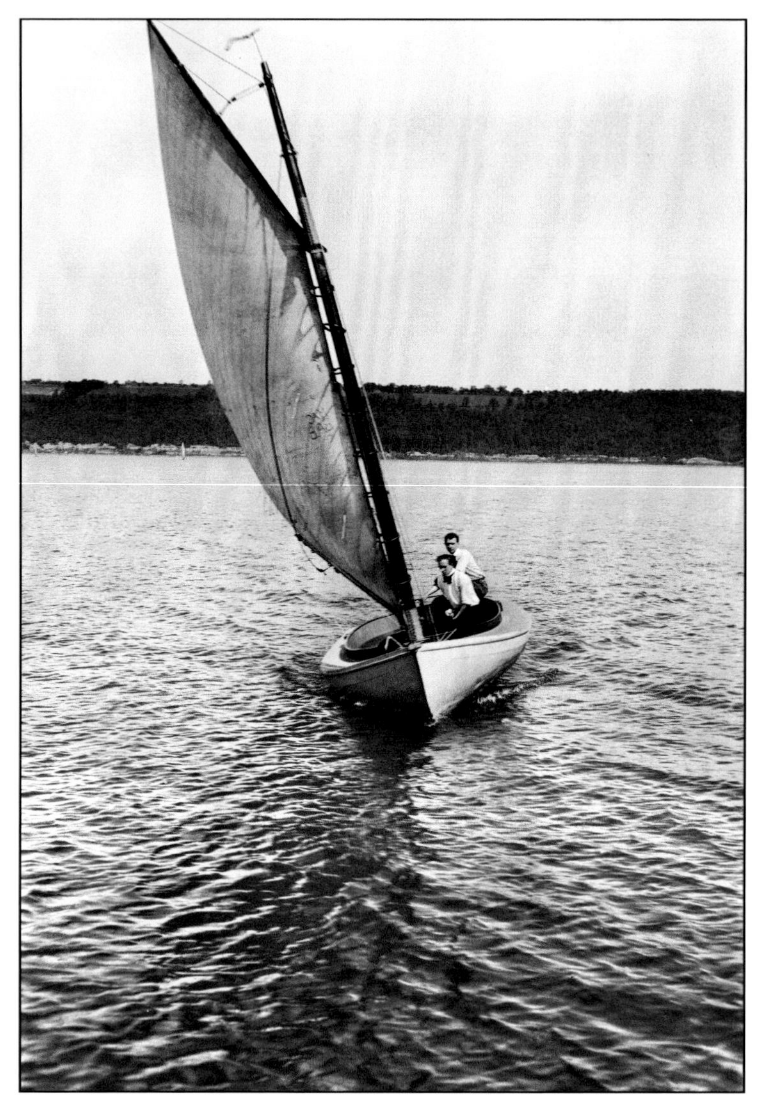

Plate 1

Accession Number: 1976.208.574 *CORNELL* sailed by H.W. Gillette and H.D. Fisher on Lake Cayuga, NY. Photo by Willis Morris.

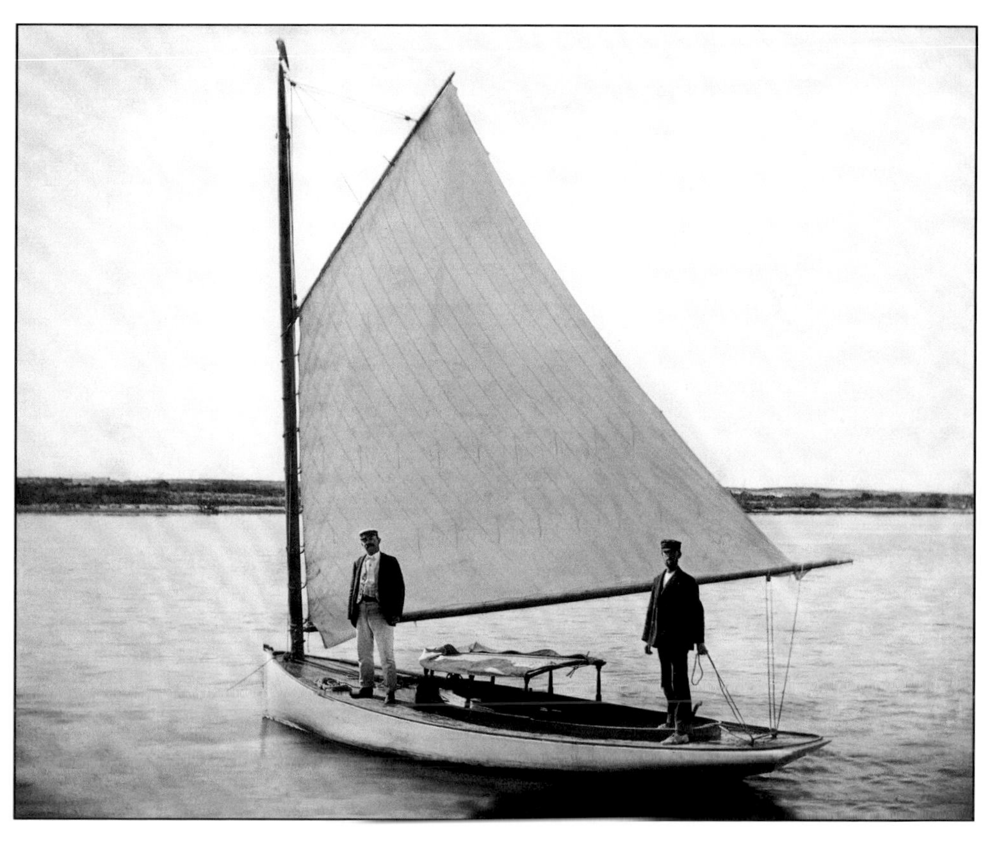

Plate 2

Accession Number: 1984.185.5 *UNIDENTIFIED* vessel. Gelatin Dryplate Negative.

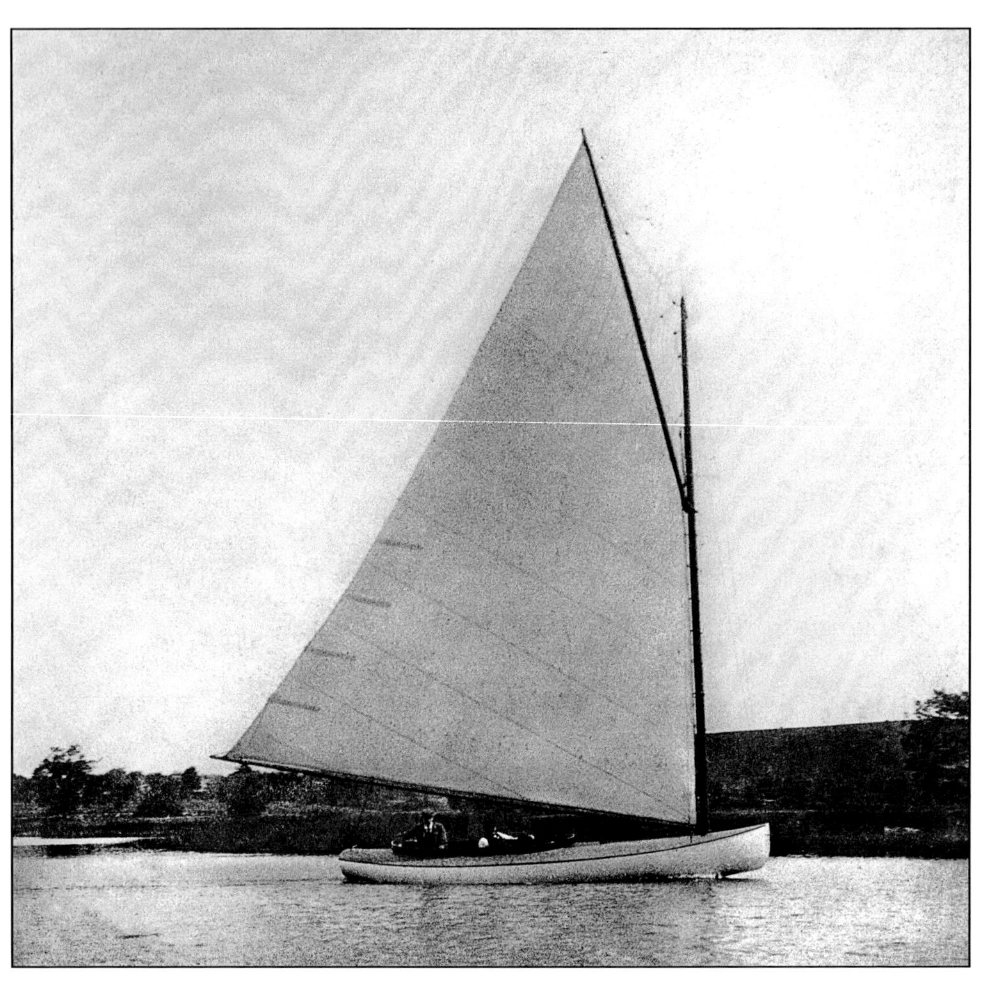

Plate 3

Accession Number: 1993.6.237 *ELIZABETH*

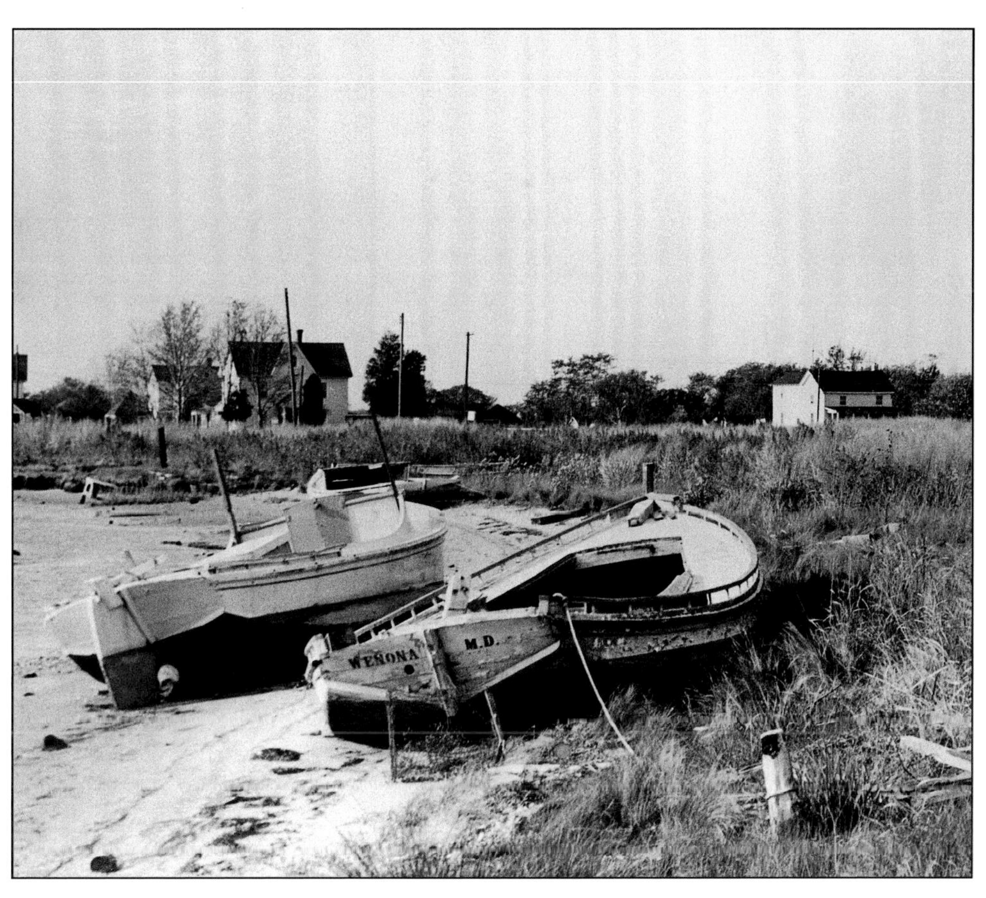

Plate 4

Accession Number: 1993.17.451 *WENONA* and *UNIDENTIFIED* vessel.

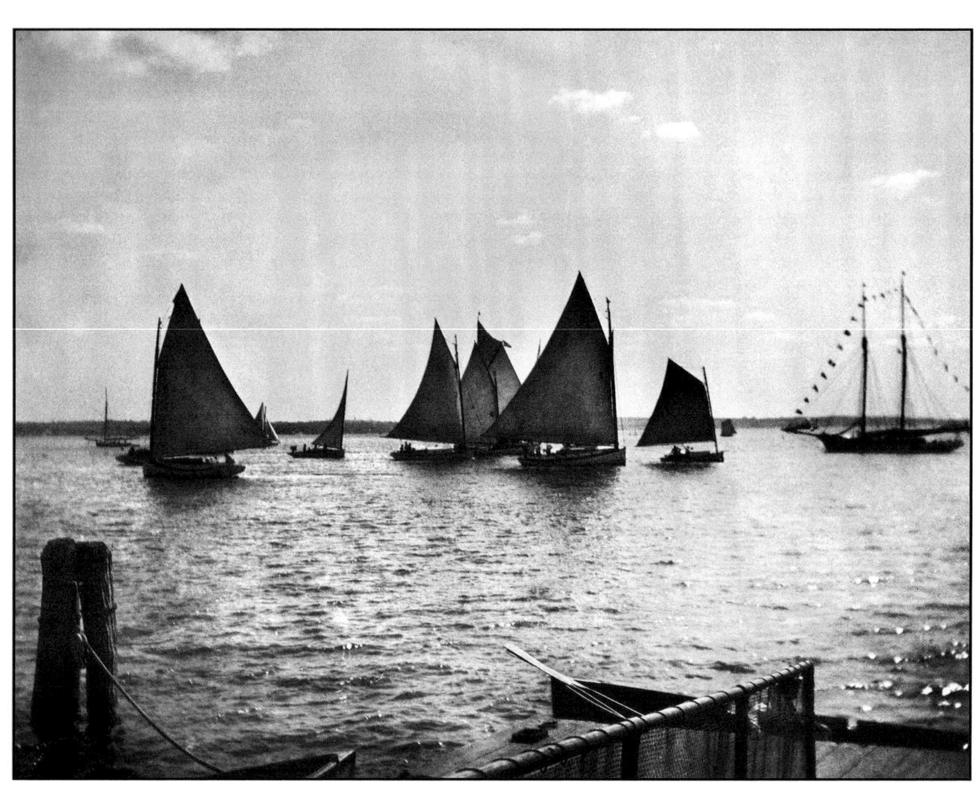

Plate 5

Accession Number: 1969.822.147 Catboat race in harbor.

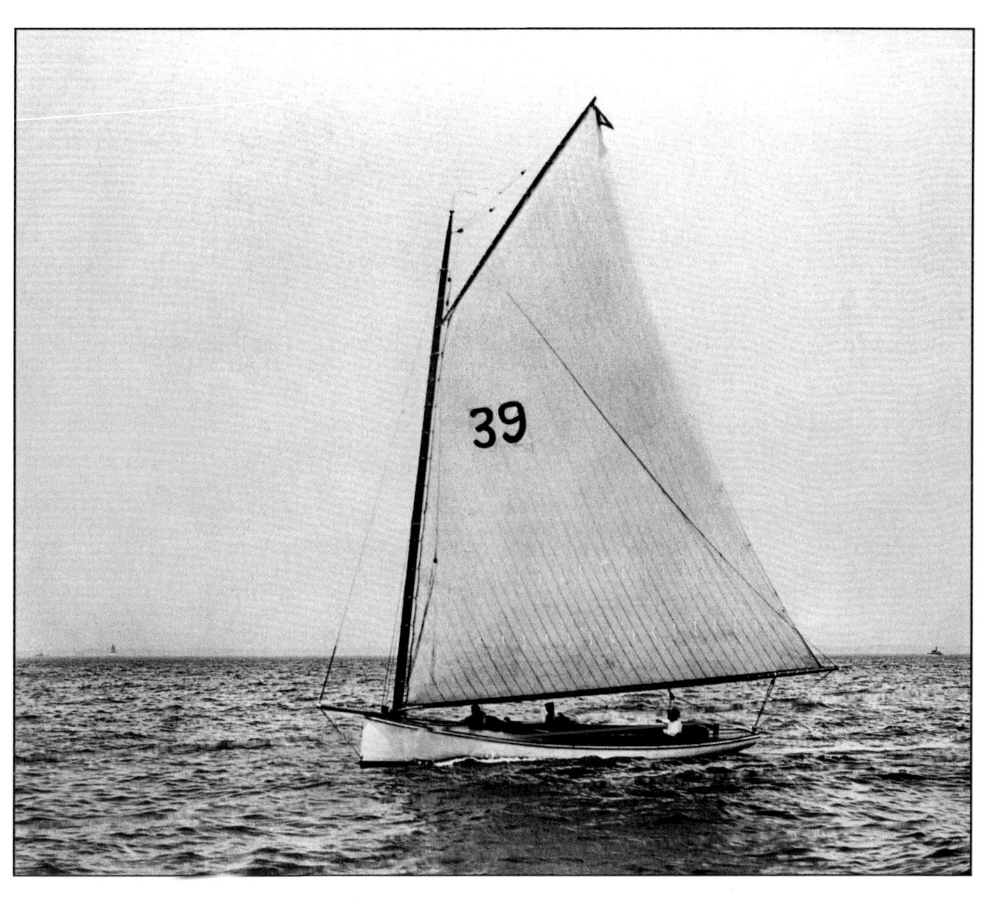

Plate 6

Accession Number: 1993.17.209 *BIJOU*

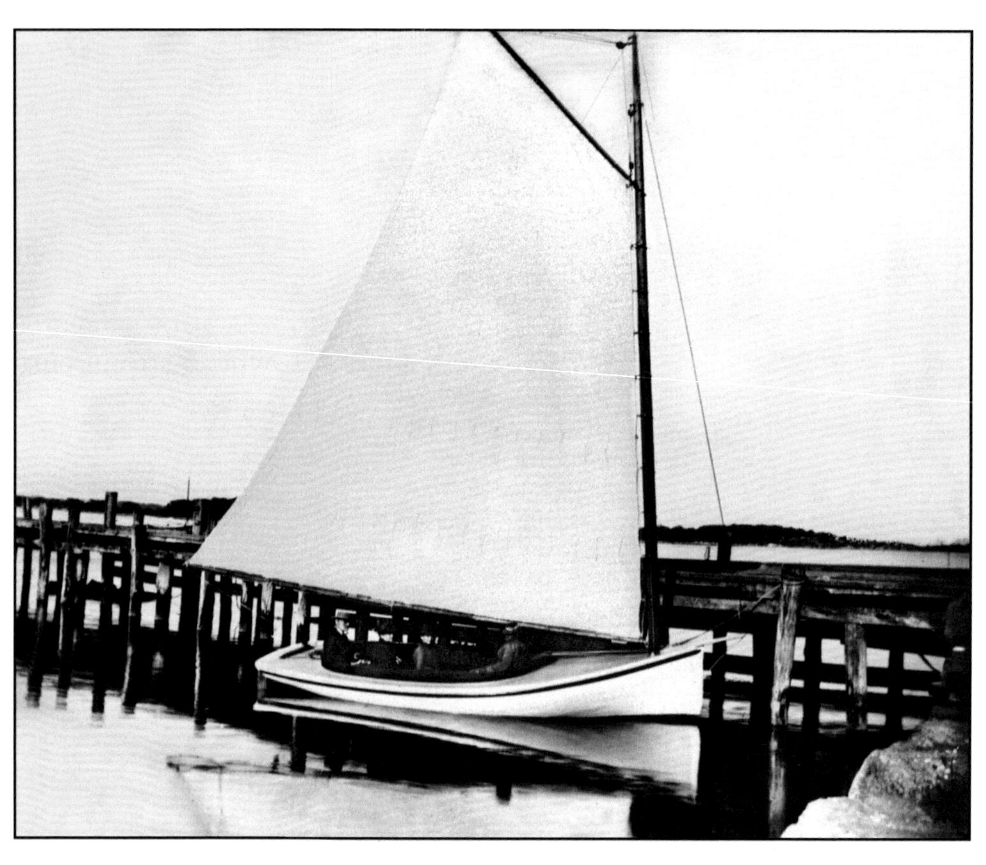

Plate 7

Accession Number: 1965.535 *GAZELLE* at the dock in Noank, CT. Silver print.

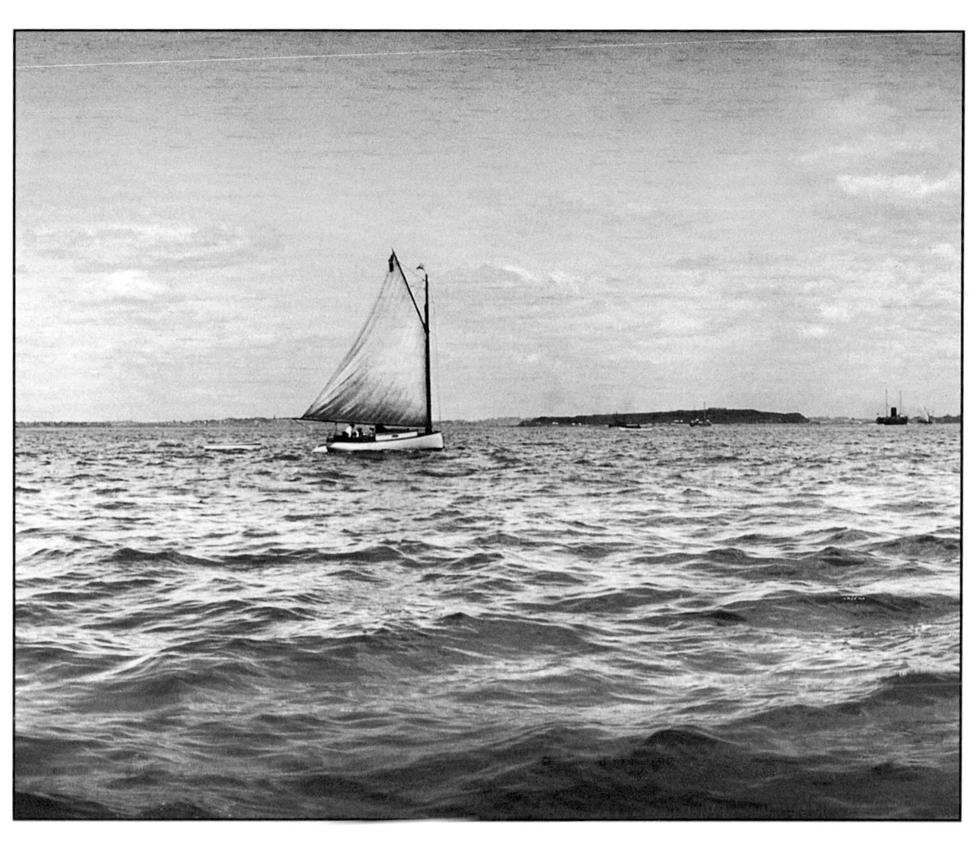

Plate 8

Accession Number: 1976.208.709 *WINTHROP* sailing.

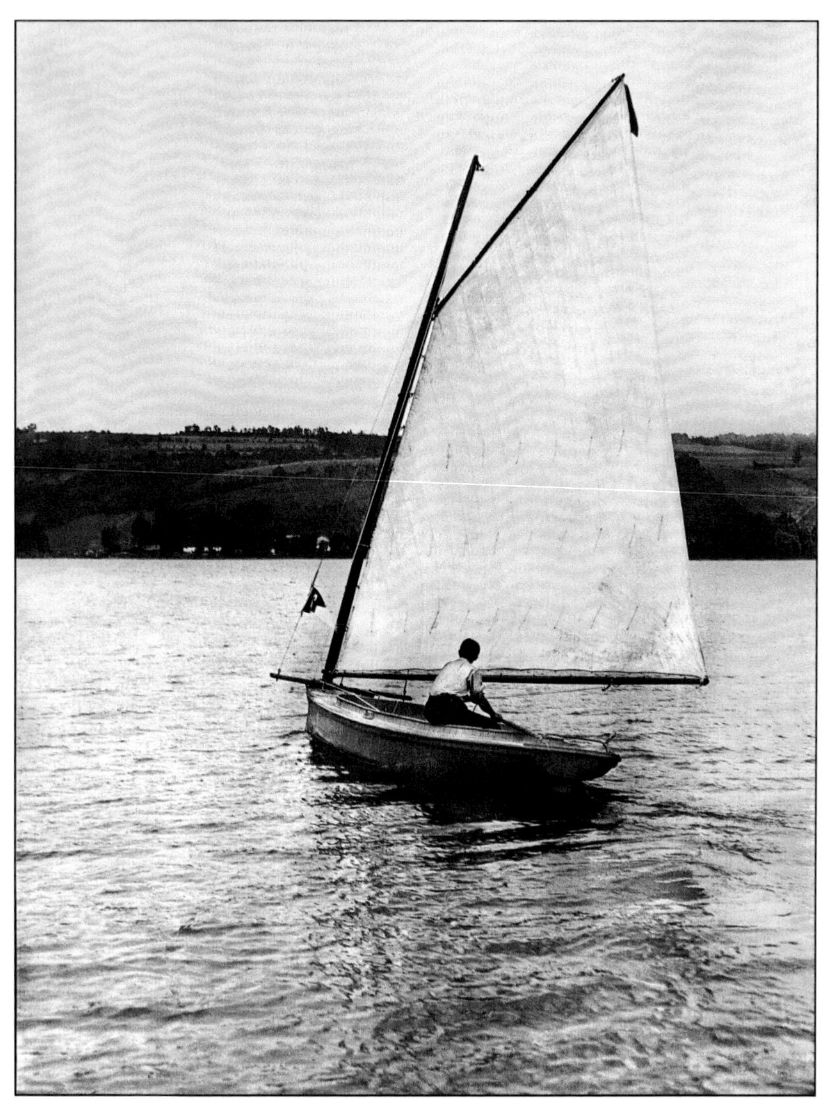

Plate 9

Accession Number: 84.97.1 Henry D. Fisher in *GEE WIZ* on lake Ogoyago in NY, September 9, 1908.

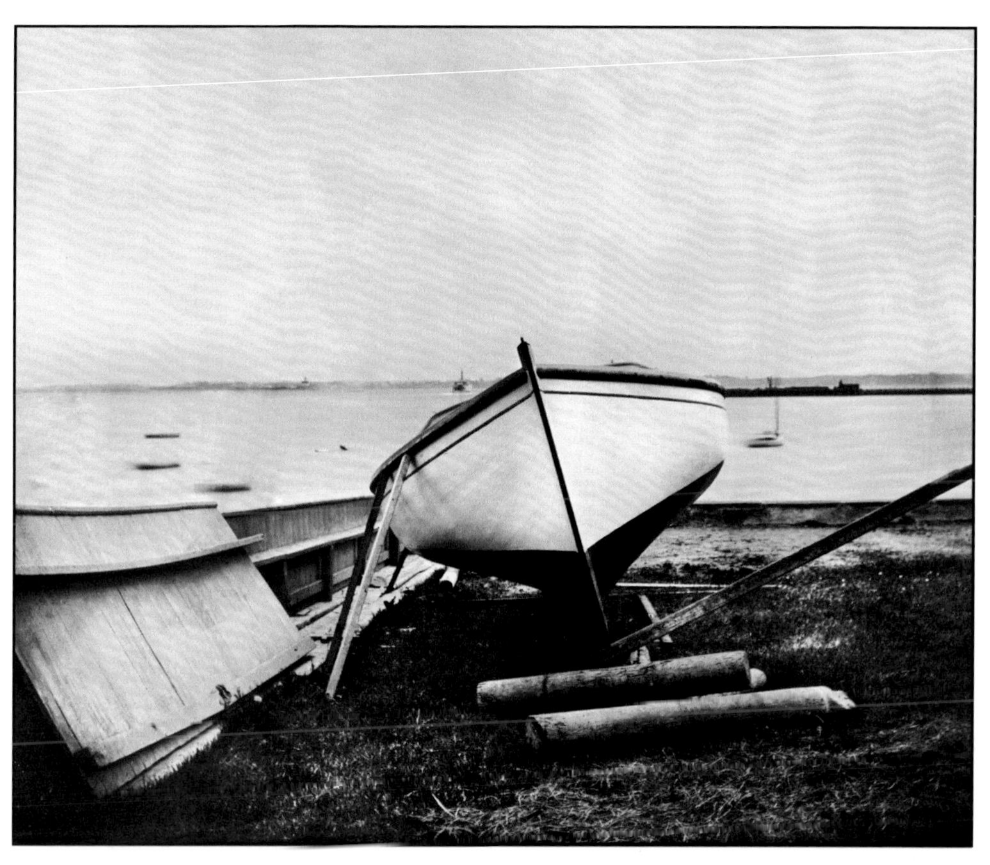

Plate 10

Accession Number: 69.822.68 *FALCON* Designed by Z. Hallett, Built by H.L. Lambert, Hyannis, Ma 1889. Photo by Edward W. Smith, ca. 1890-1905. Gelatin Glass Plate. Vessel size: 25' x 11' 9" x 3'

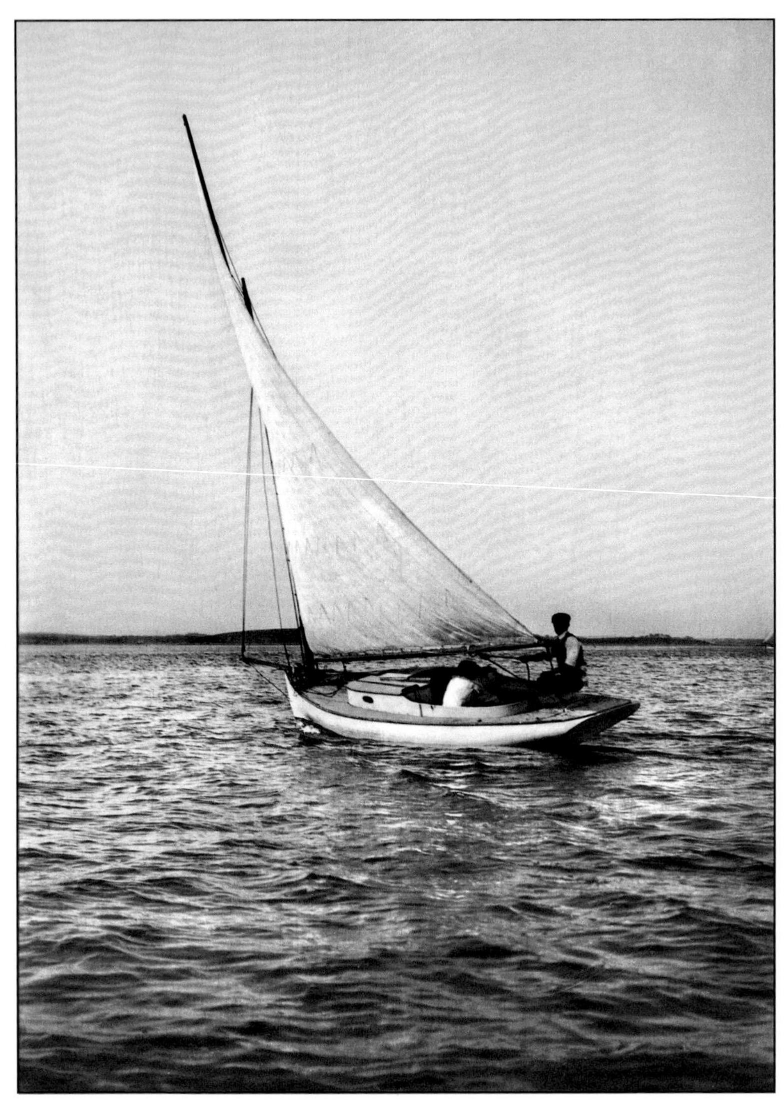

Plate 11

Accession Number: 1976.208.338 *UNIDENTIFIED* vessel.
Henry D. Fisher Collection.

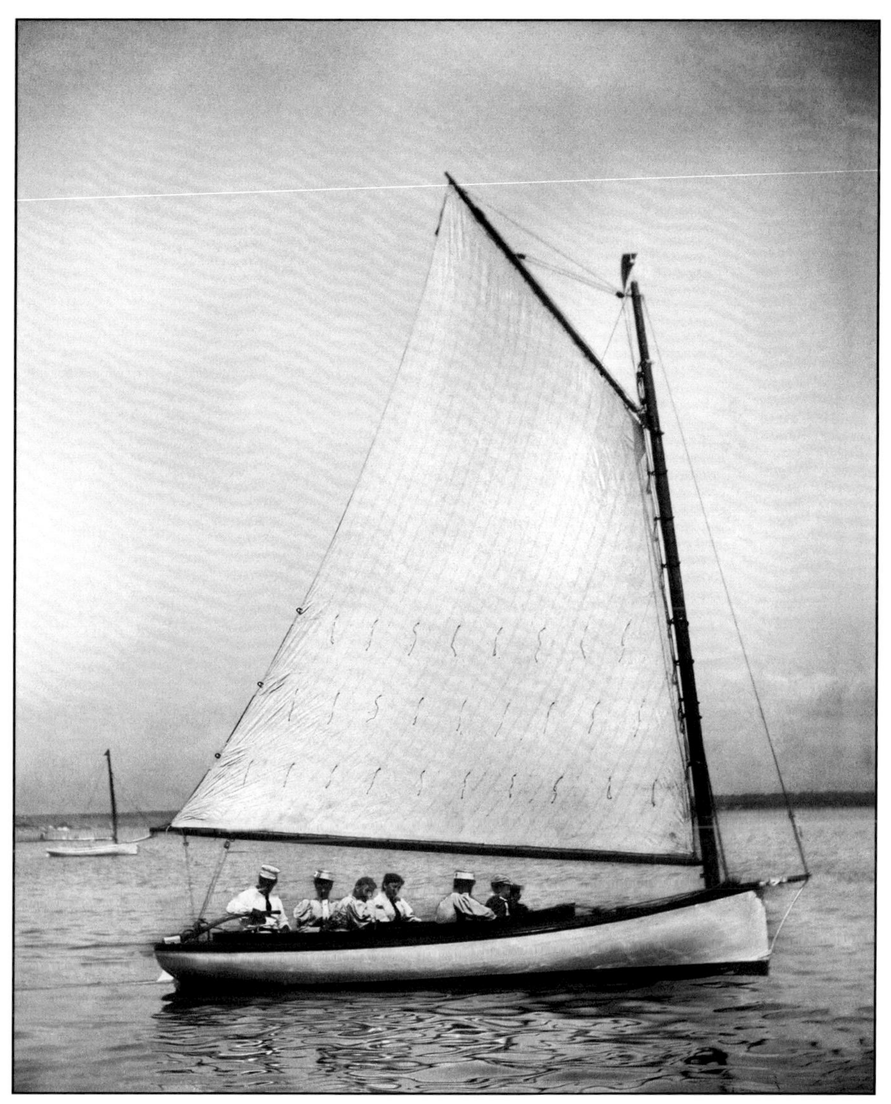

Plate 12

Accession Number: 1969.822.191 *UNIDENTIFIED* vessel. Photograph ca. 1890-1905 by Edward W. Smith. Gelatin glass plate negative.

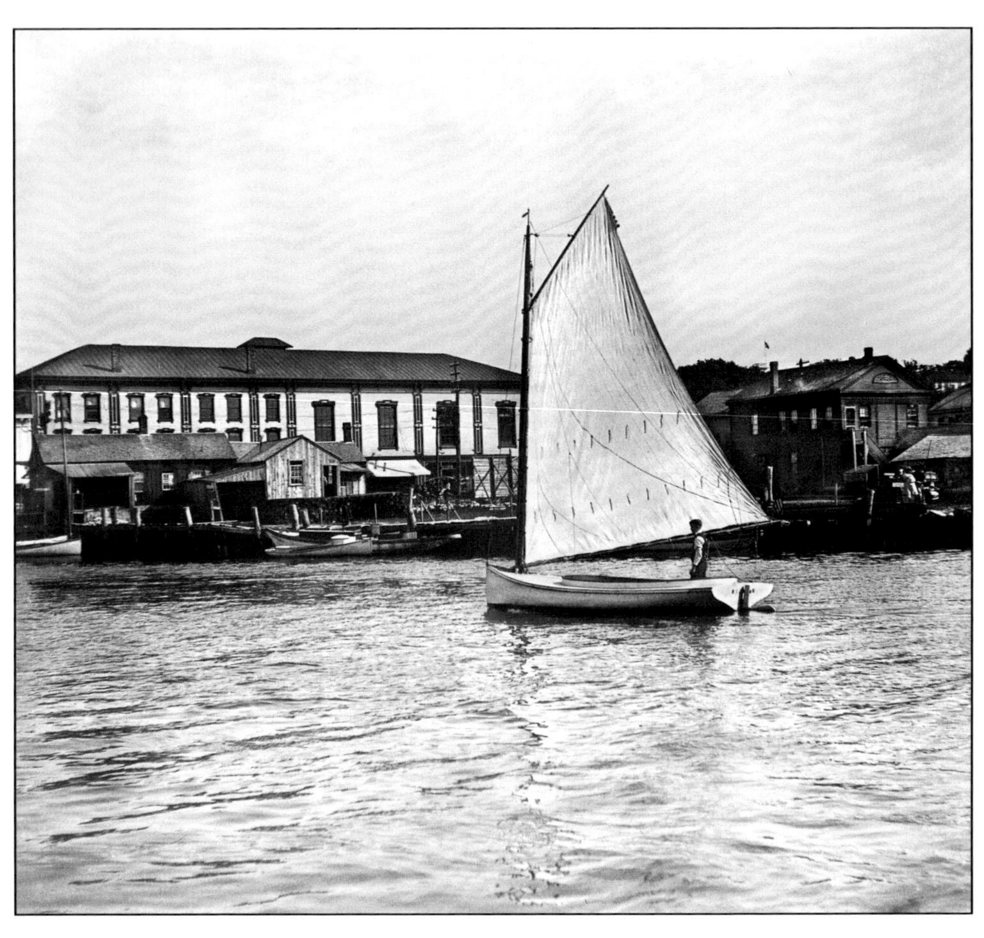

Plate 13

Accession Number: 1983.57.201 *UNIDENTIFIED* vessel on the Mystic River, CT. Photograph by G. Victor Grinnell. Gelatin glass plate negative.

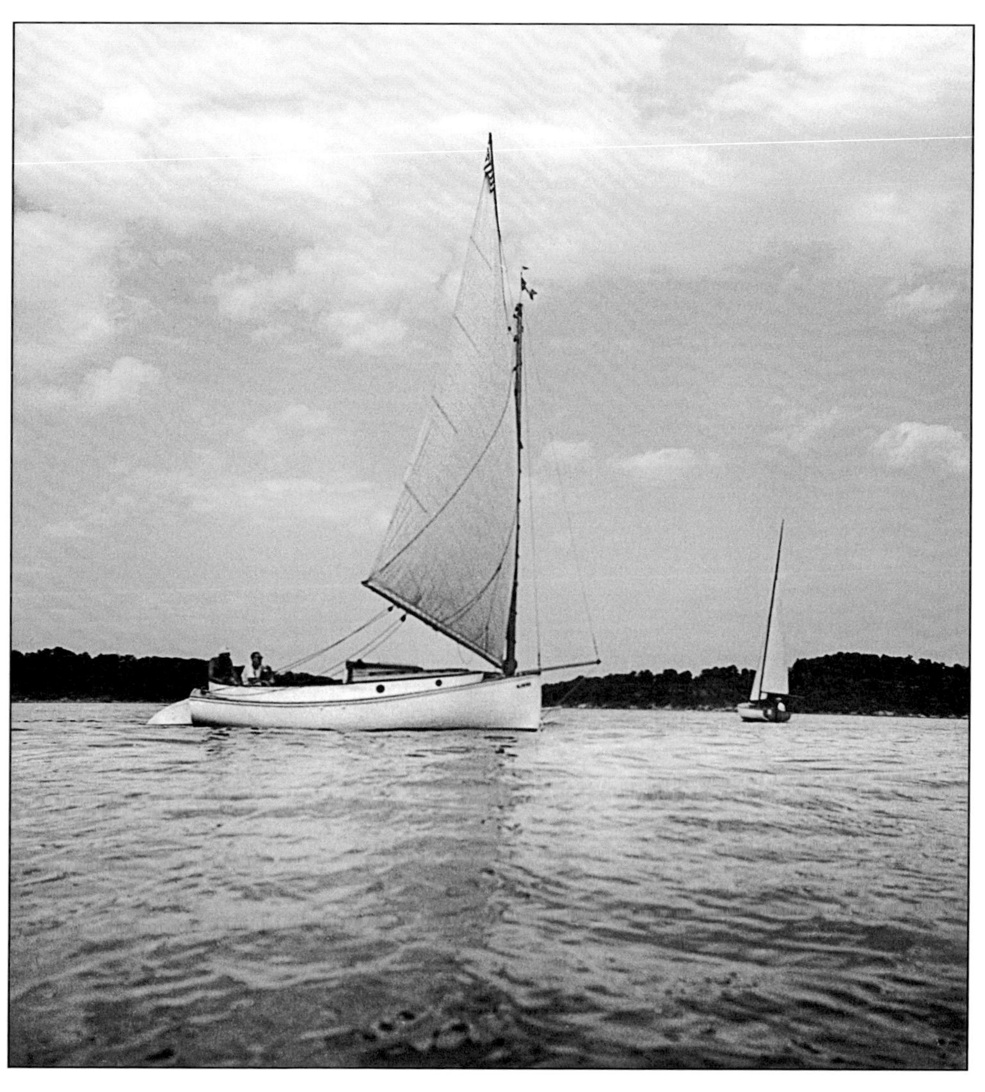

Plate 14

Accession Number: 1986.16.753 *CHEE CHITA* sailing near Hingham MA, 1954.

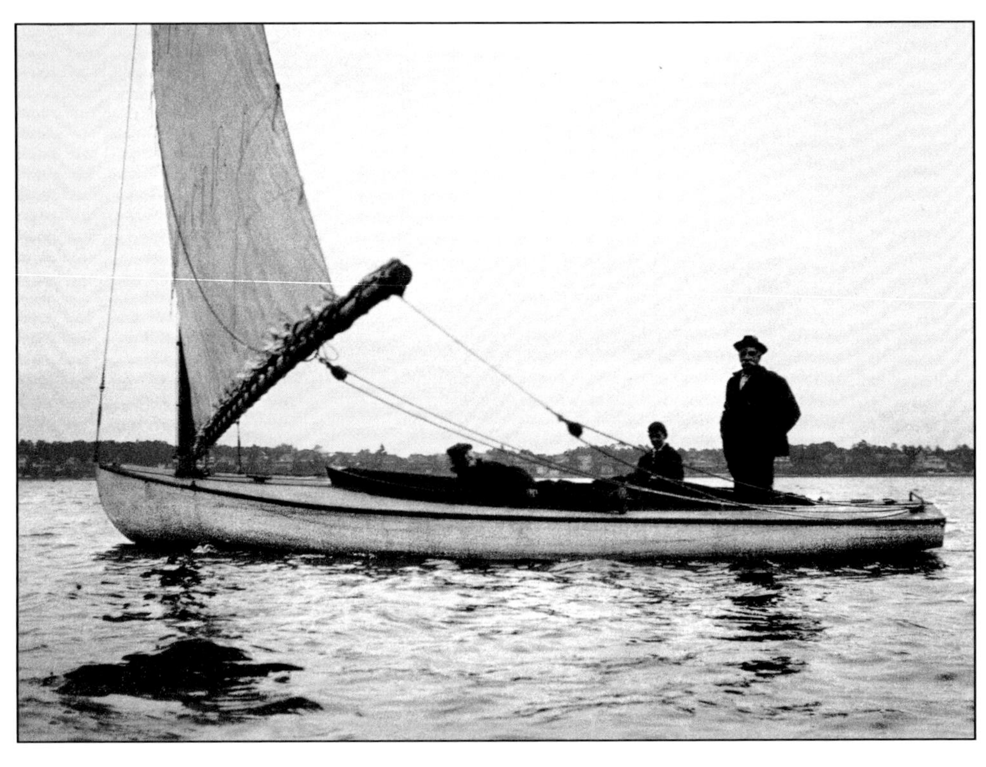

Plate 15

Accession Number: 1990.67.150 *RASCAL* running before the wind on October 4, 1919. Budlong Family Album.

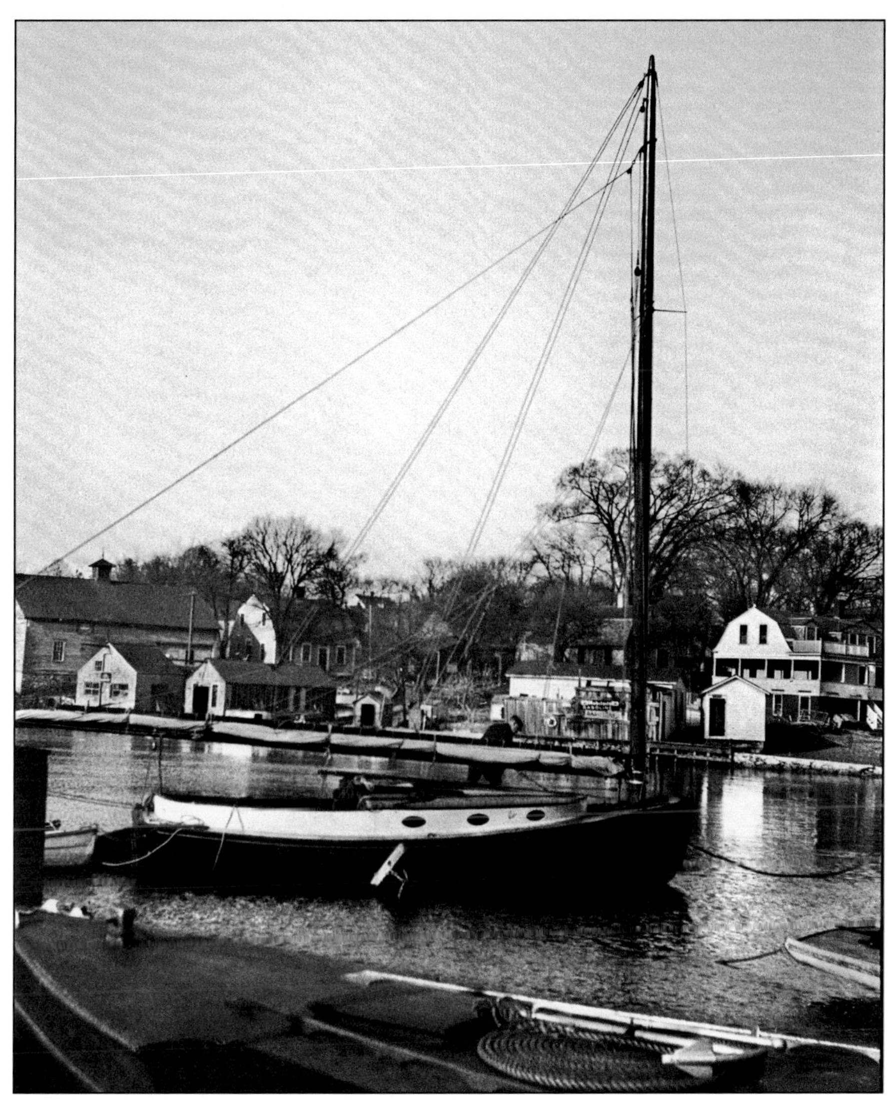

Plate 16

Accession Number: 1990.67.34 *ALMA* at rest in Pawtuxet Cove, RI. 1919
Nitrate negative.

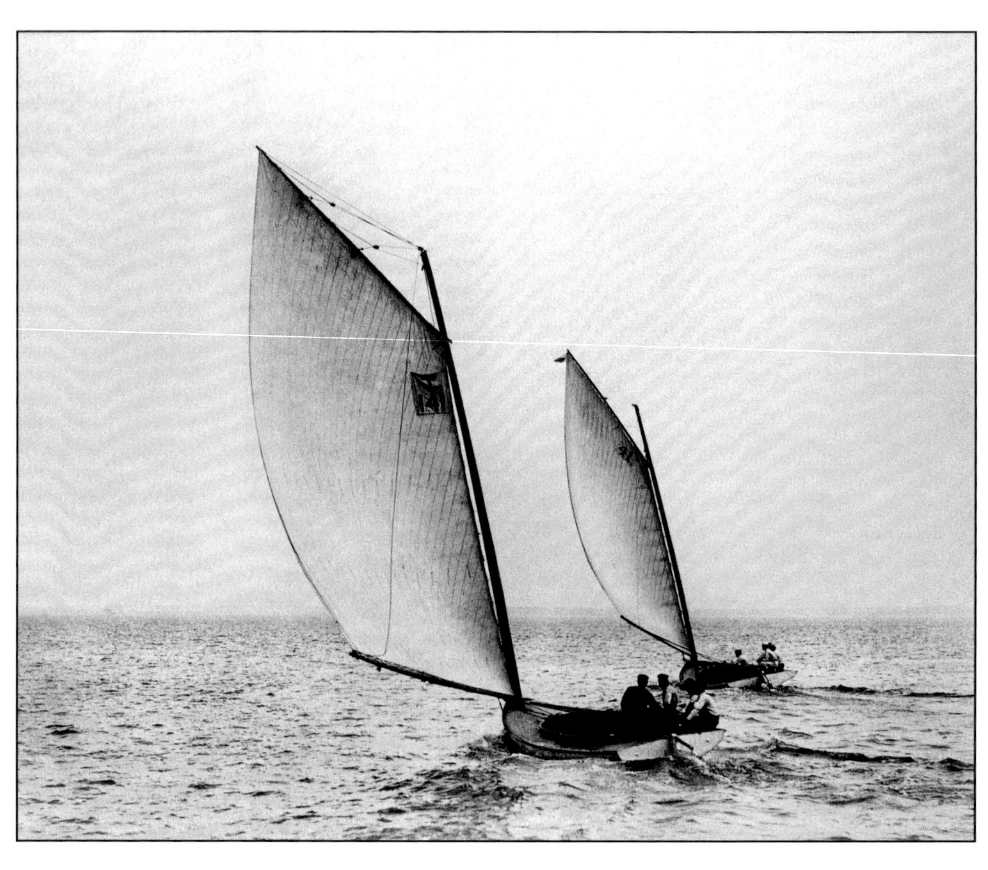

Plate 17

Accession Number: 1993.17.227 *OSPREY* and *SIRENE* running downwind.

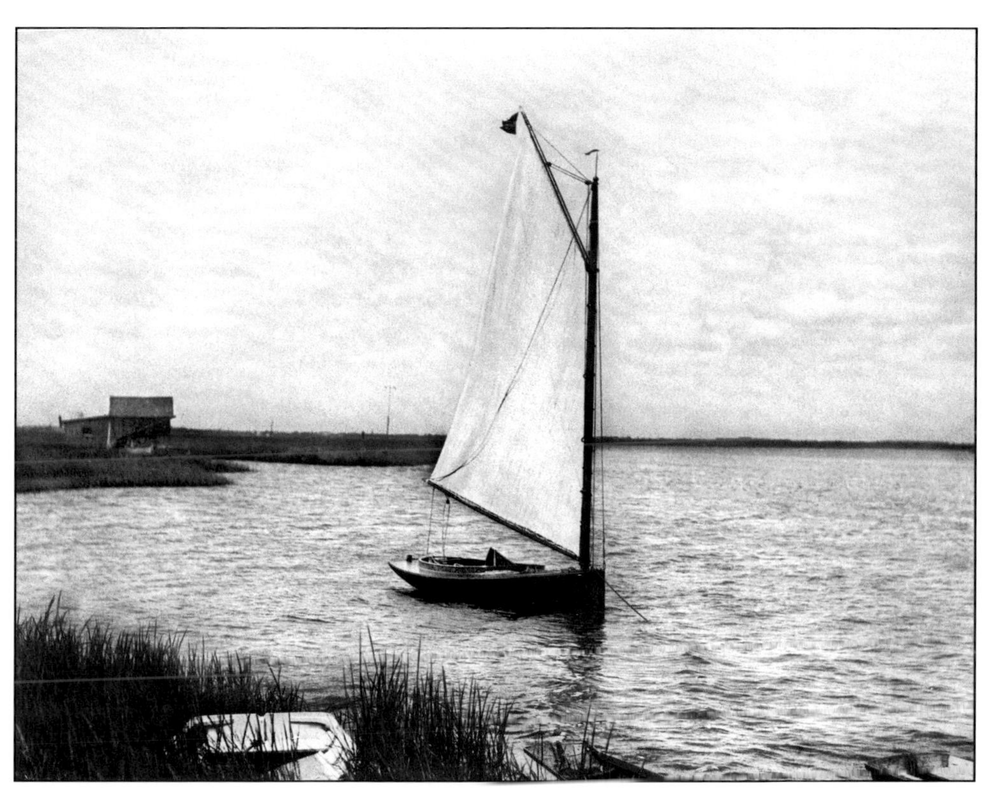

Plate 18

Accession Number: 1990.29.16 *UNIDENTIFIED* vessel.
Barrnegat Bay or Great South Bay style catboat at anchor.

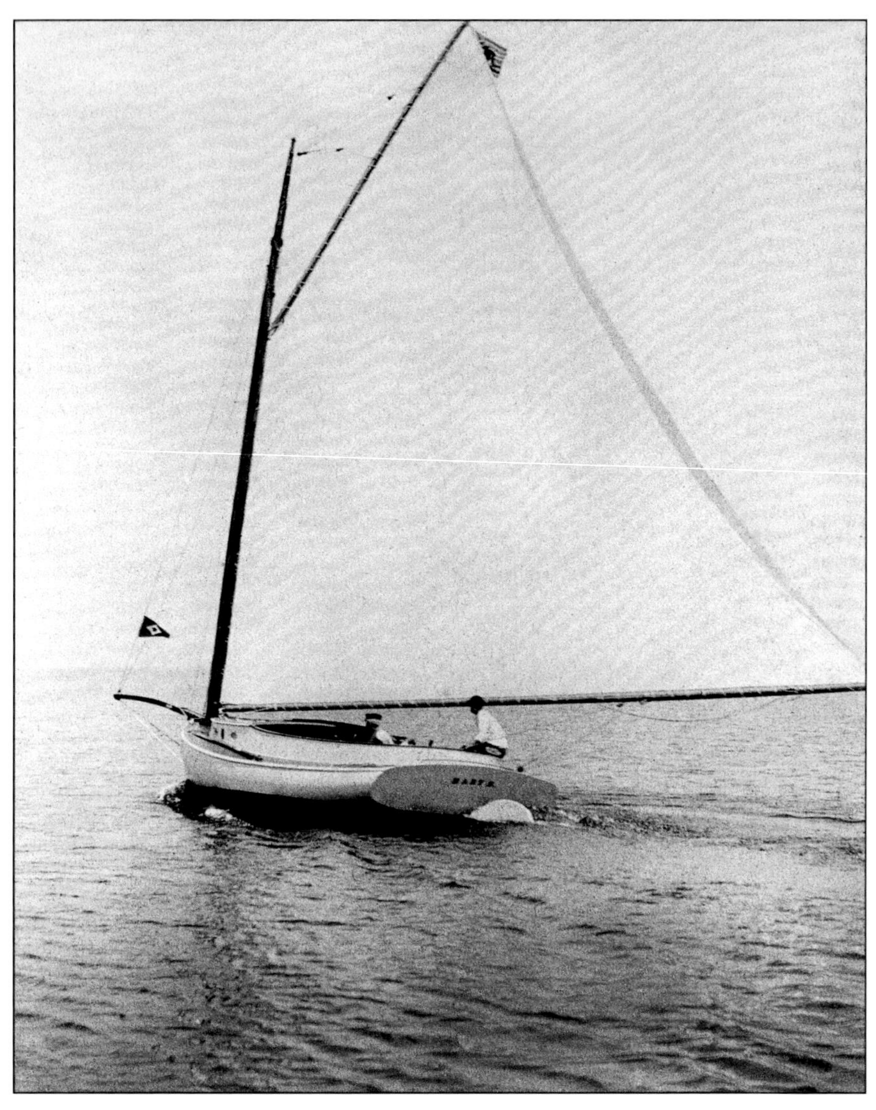

Plate 19

Accession Number: 1993.6.211 *MARY S*

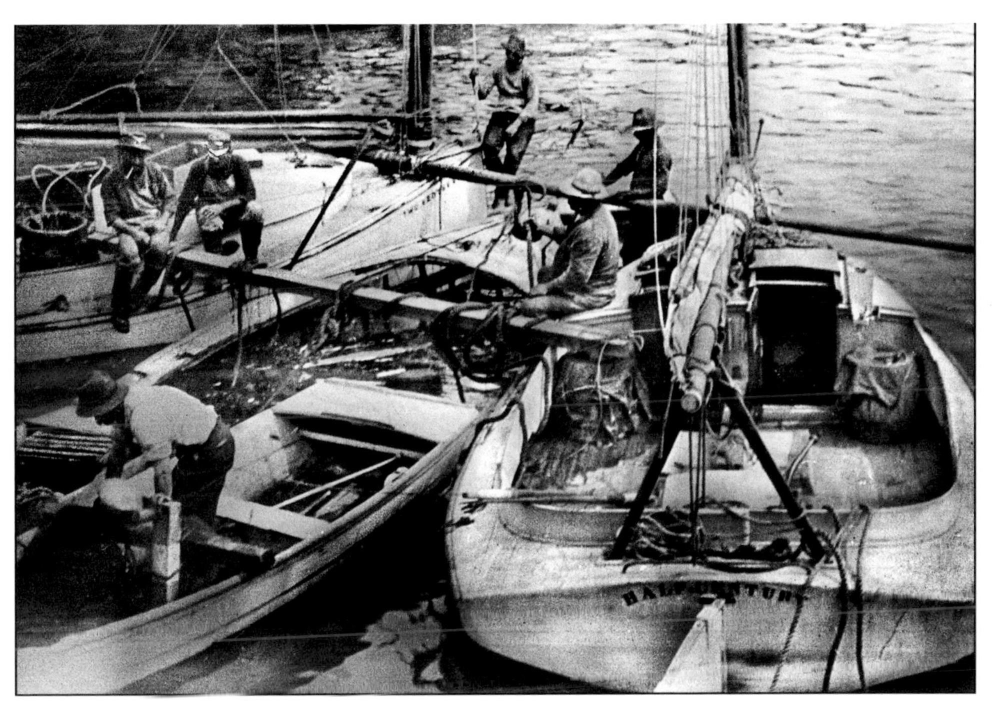

Plate 20

Accession Number: 1982.84.30 *HALF CENTURY* and *TWO BROTHERS* raise a sunken vessel at the dock.

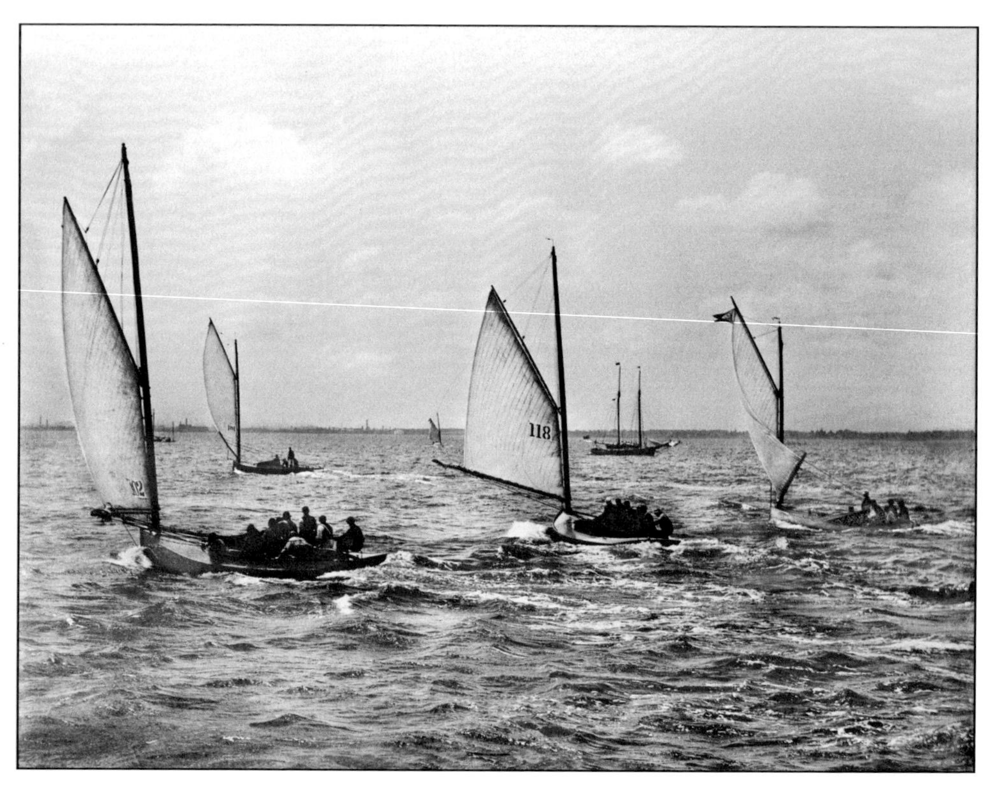

Plate 21

Accession Number: 1993.17.205 *MAY F., HENRY DAUER, & HOMING* racing in a harbor in 1891.

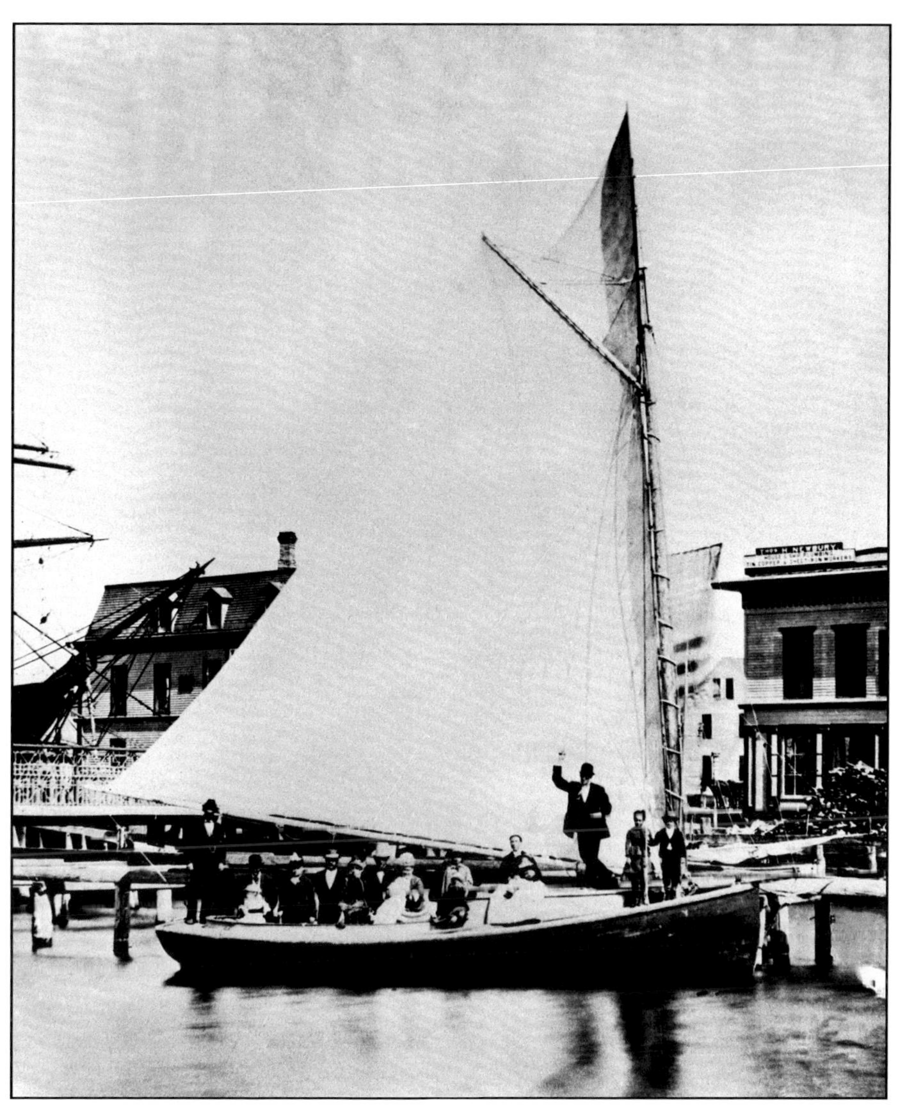

Plate 22

Accession Number: 1976.166.13 *UNIDENTIFIED* vessel at the dock on the Mystic River, CT. Photograph by E.A Scholfield. Glass plate negative.

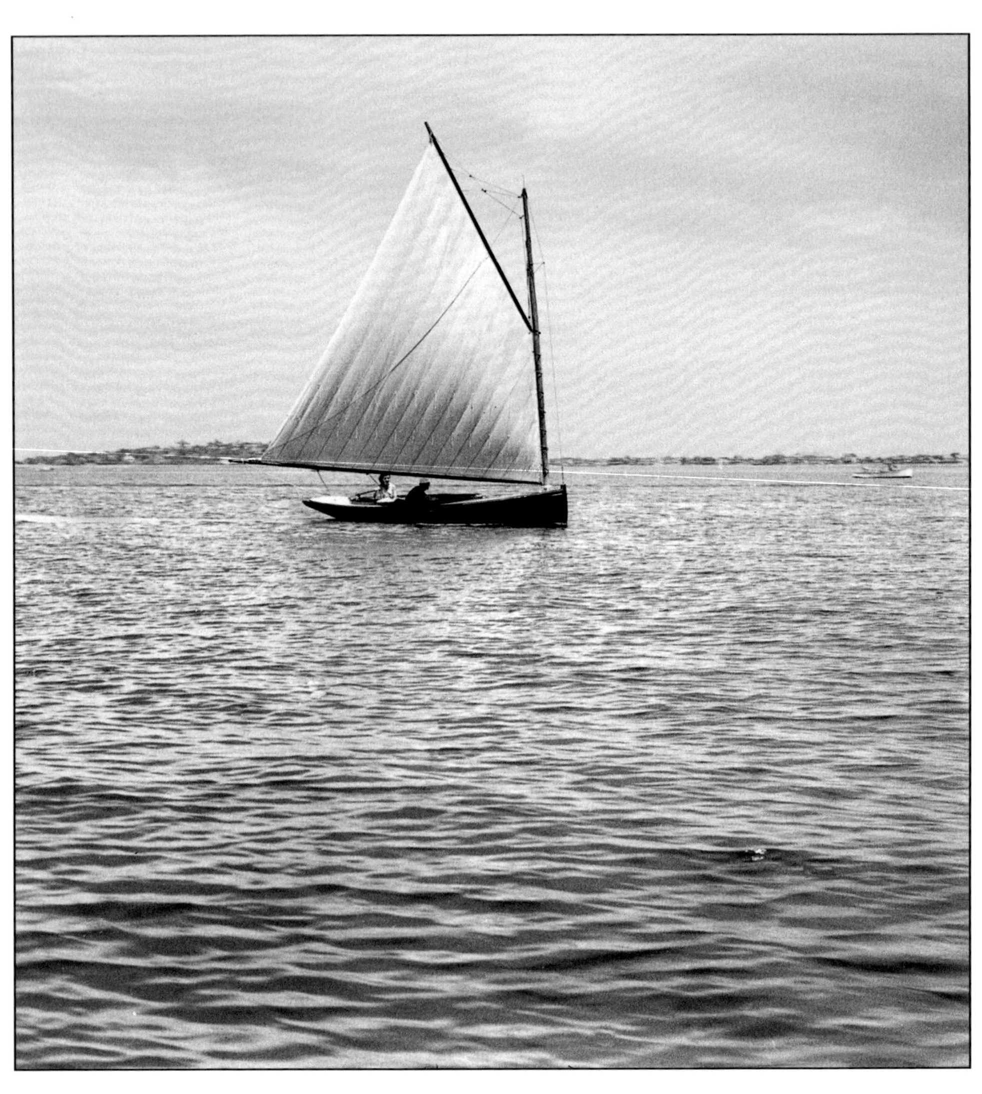

Plate 23

Accession Number: 1986.16.626 *UNIDENTIFIED* Herreshoff catboat.

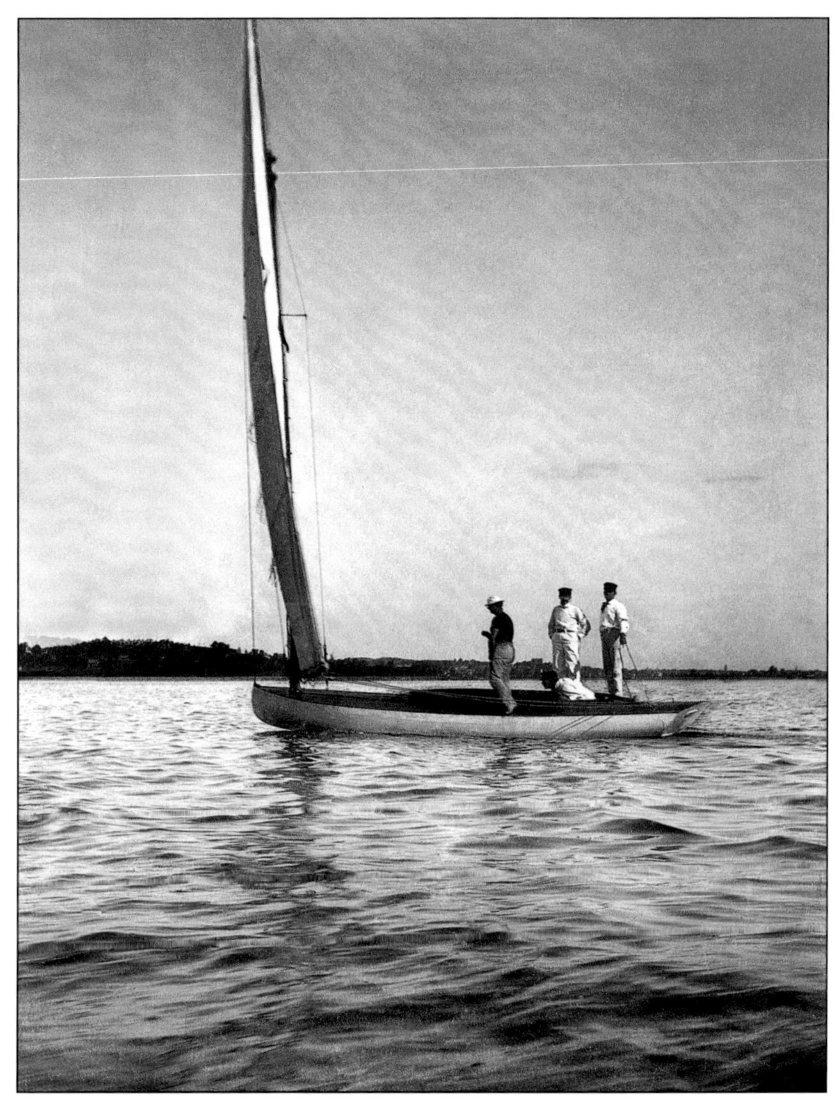

Plate 24

Accession Number: 1969.822.162 *UNIDENTIFIED* vessel ghosting along. Photograph ca. 1890-1905 by Edward W. Smith. Gelatin glass plate negative.

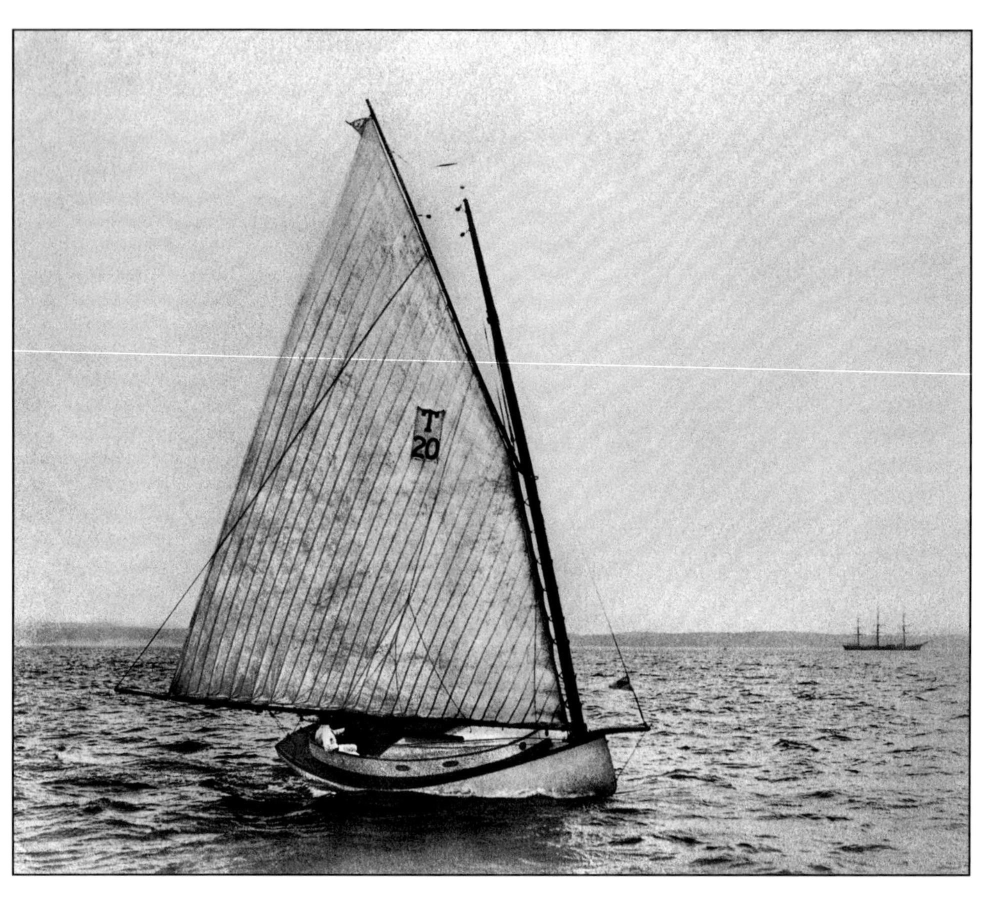

Plate 25

Accession Number: 1993.17.207 *GRACE* on port tack.

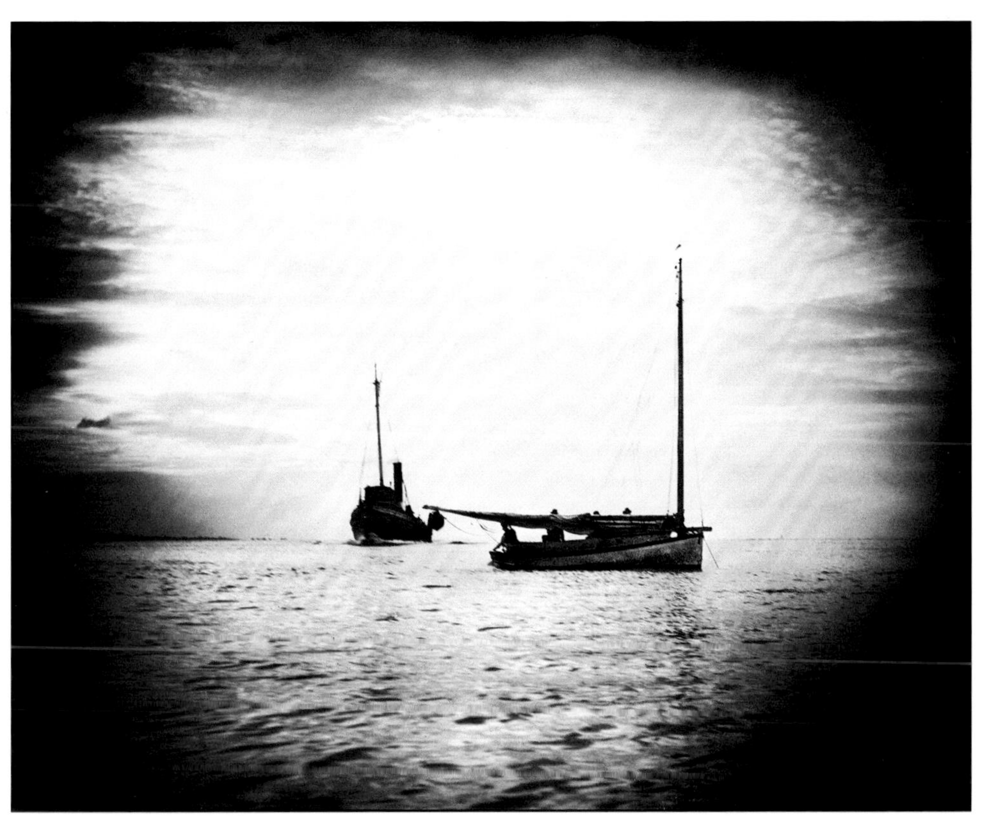

Plate 26

Accession Number: 1969.822.149 *UNIDENTIFIED* catboat and menhaden steamer off Castle Hill. Photograph ca. 1890-1905 by Edward W. Smith. Gelatin glass plate negative.

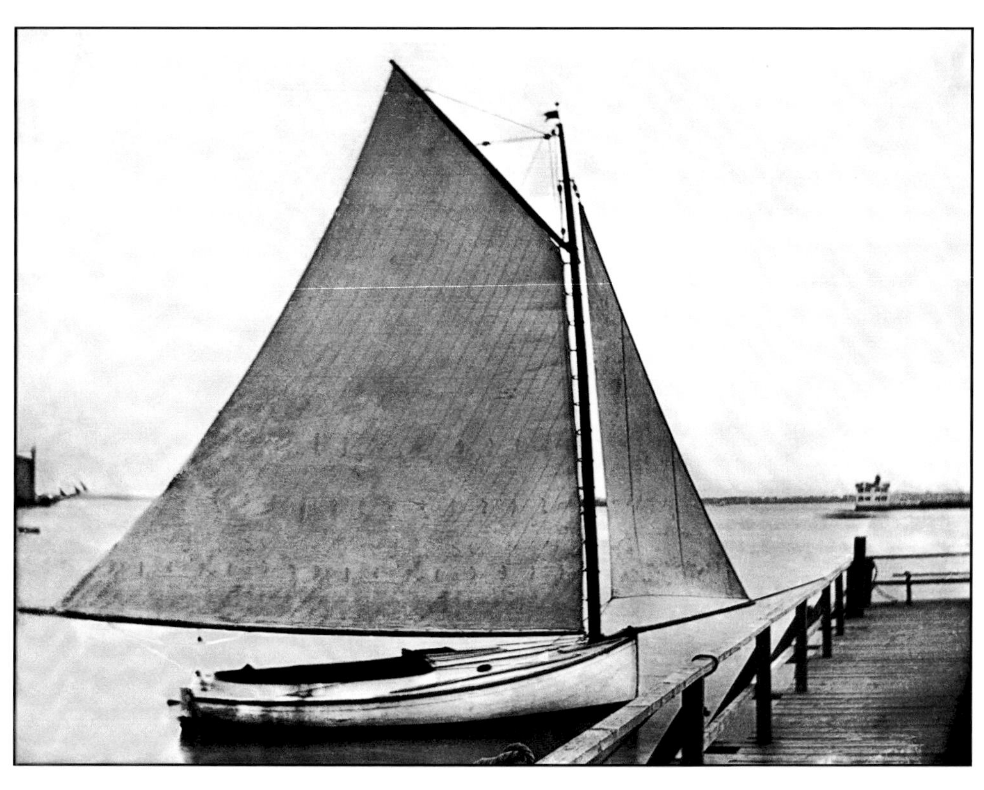

Plate 27

Accession Number: 1969.822.162 *UNIDENTIFIED* vessel at the dock.

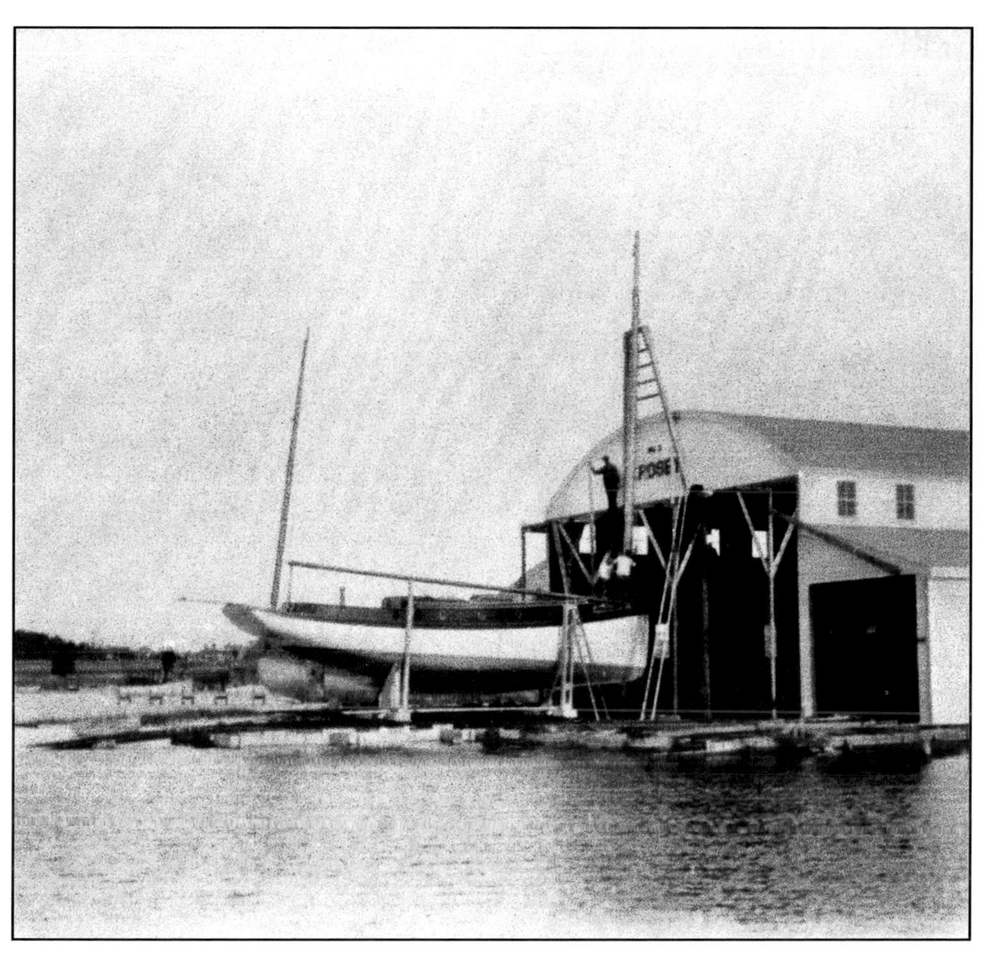

Plate 28

Accession Number: 1977.6.268 *TOSHIE NORRIE*
Cat-ketch on the ways at the Crosby shop.

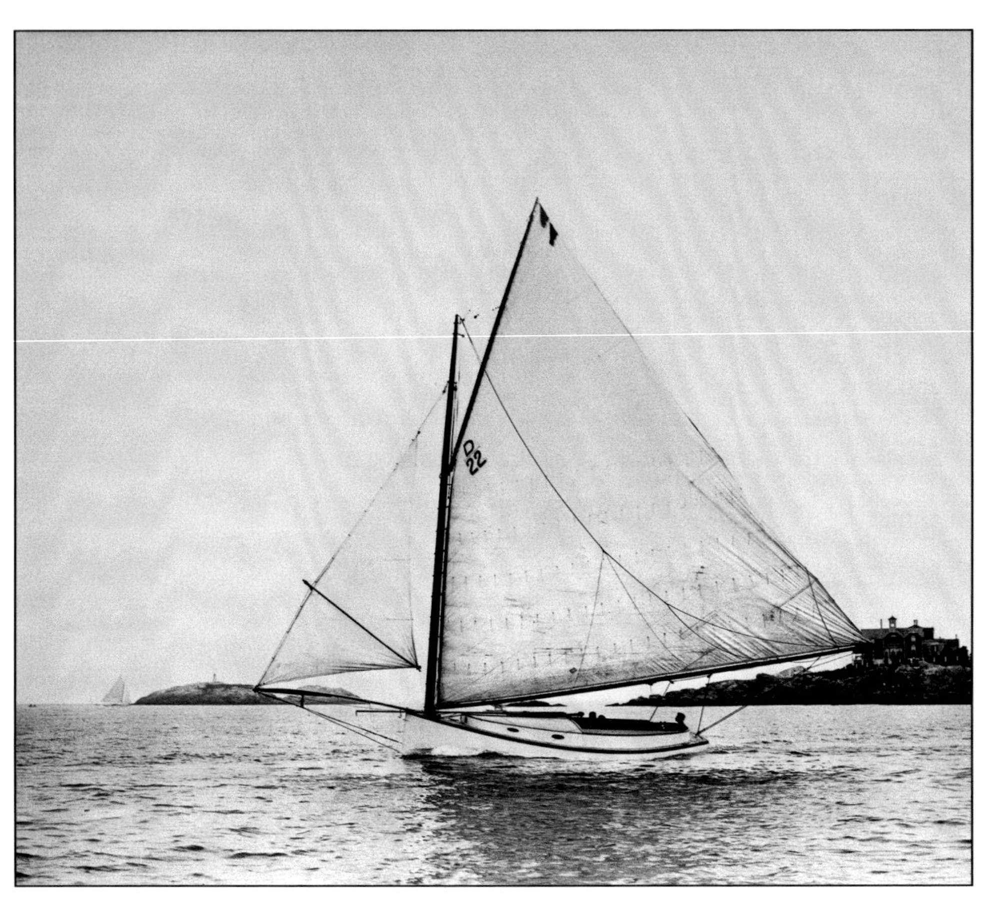

Plate 29

Accession Number: 1990.37.927 *MARVEL* Photograph probably taken by W. B. Jackson.

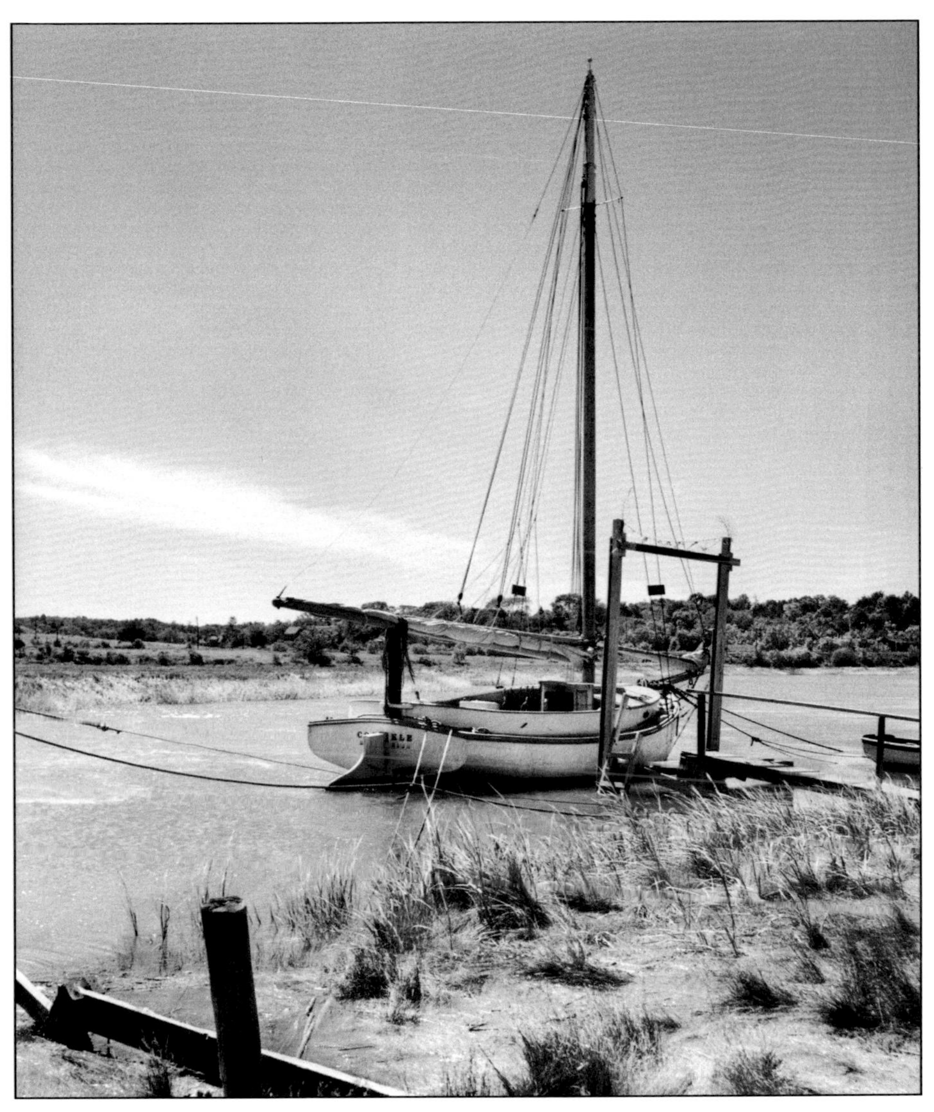

Plate 30

Accession Number: 1986.16.650 *COCKLE* on the Jones River, Kingston. Photograph by William Baker.

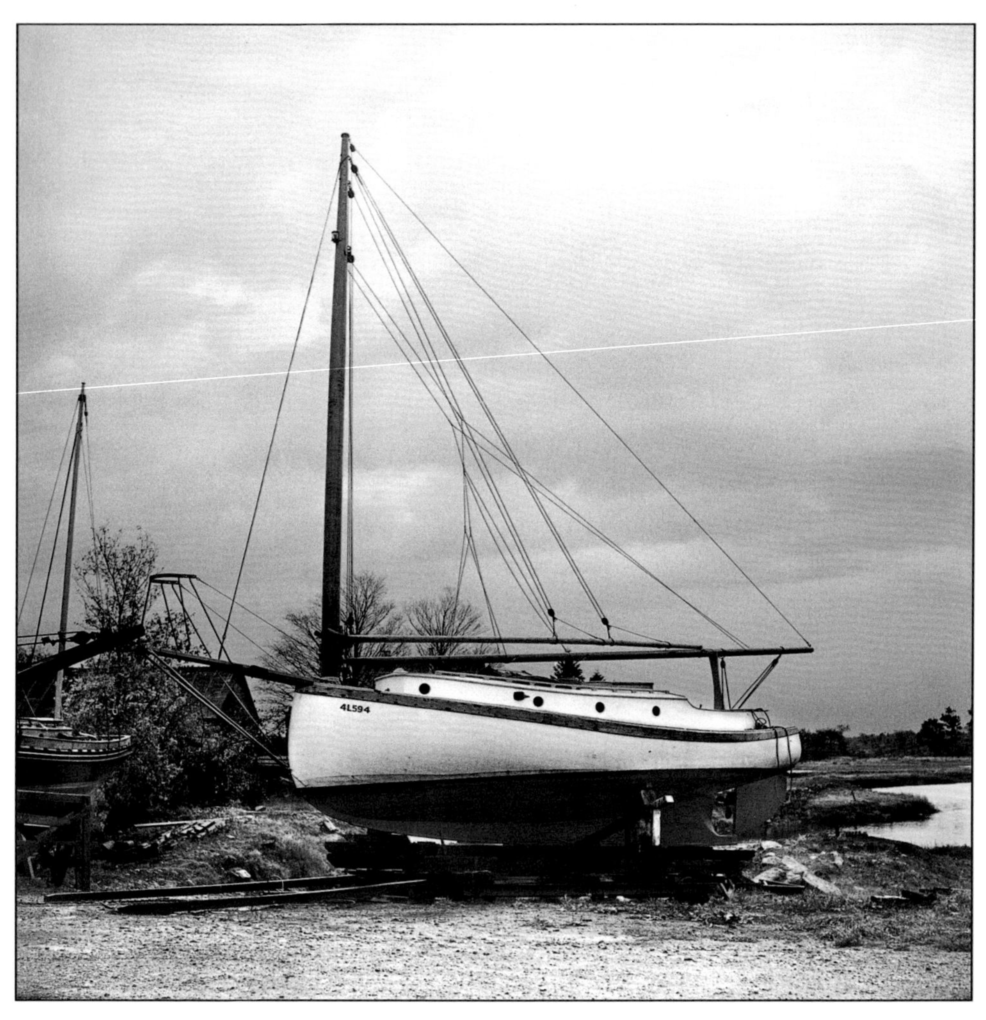

Plate 31

Accession Number: 1986.16.775 *PEDAGOGUE II.* Hauled in Essex, MA in 1954. Note bow pulpit for harpooning fish.

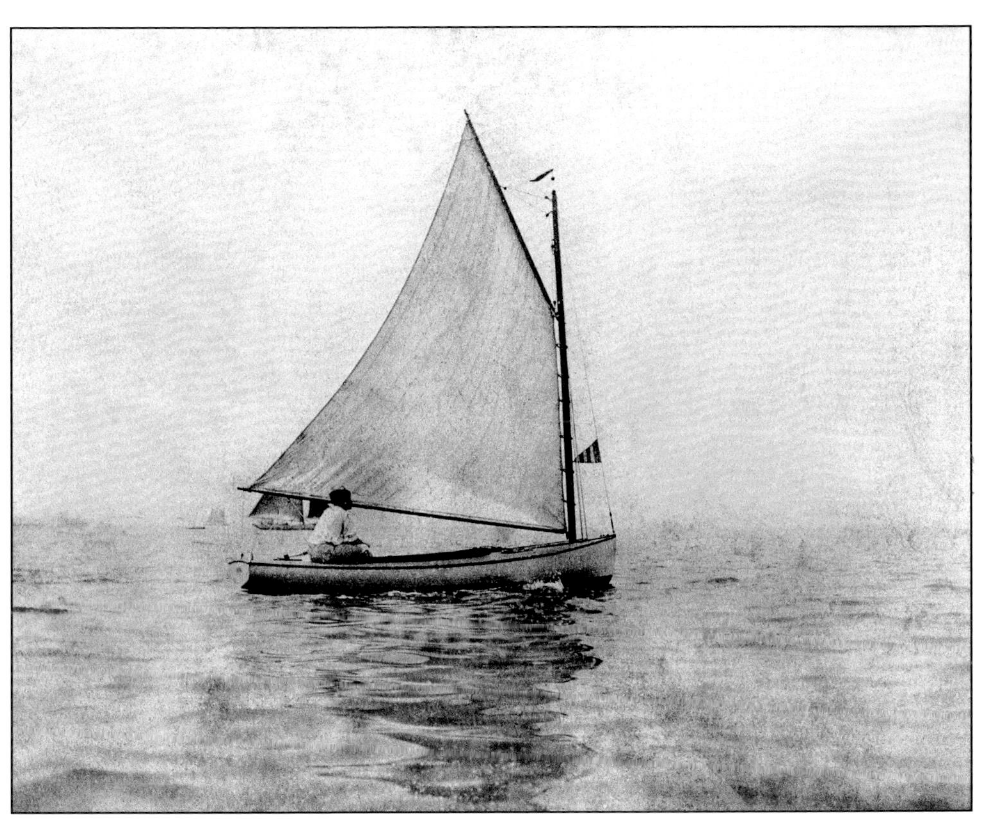

Plate 32

Accession Number: 1993.6.190 *BETH*

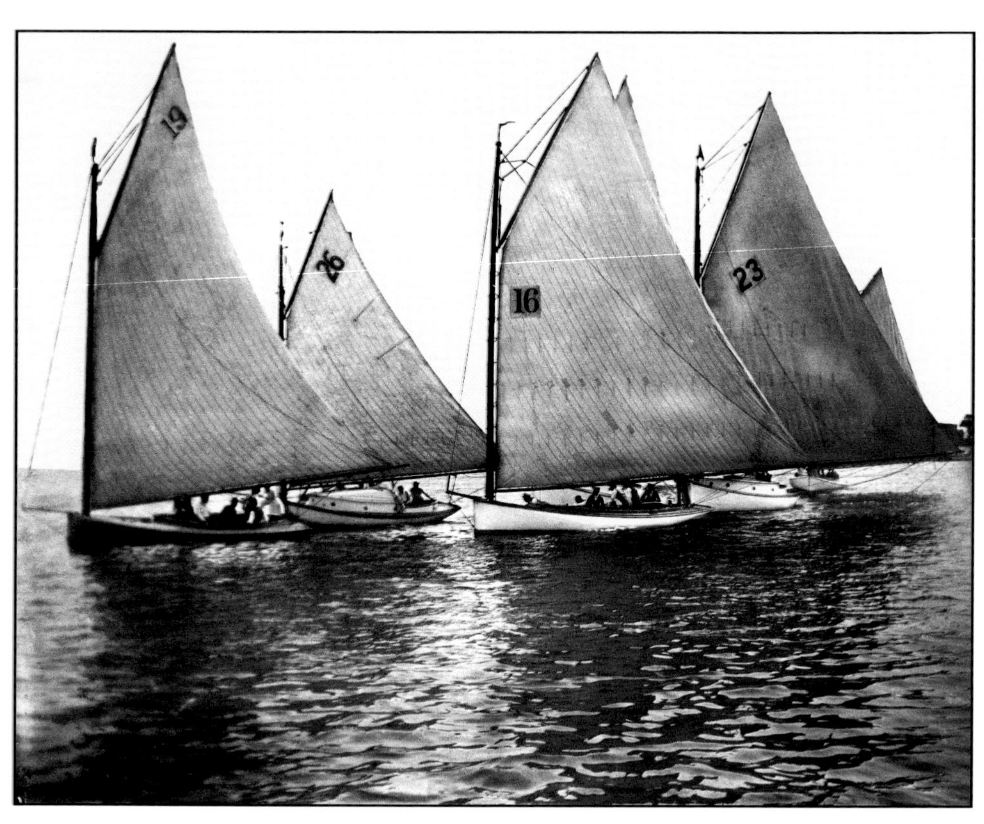

Plate 33

Accession Number: 1969.822.158 *UNIDENTIFIED* catboats racing.
Photograph ca. 1890-1905 by Edward W. Smith. Gelatin glass plate negative.

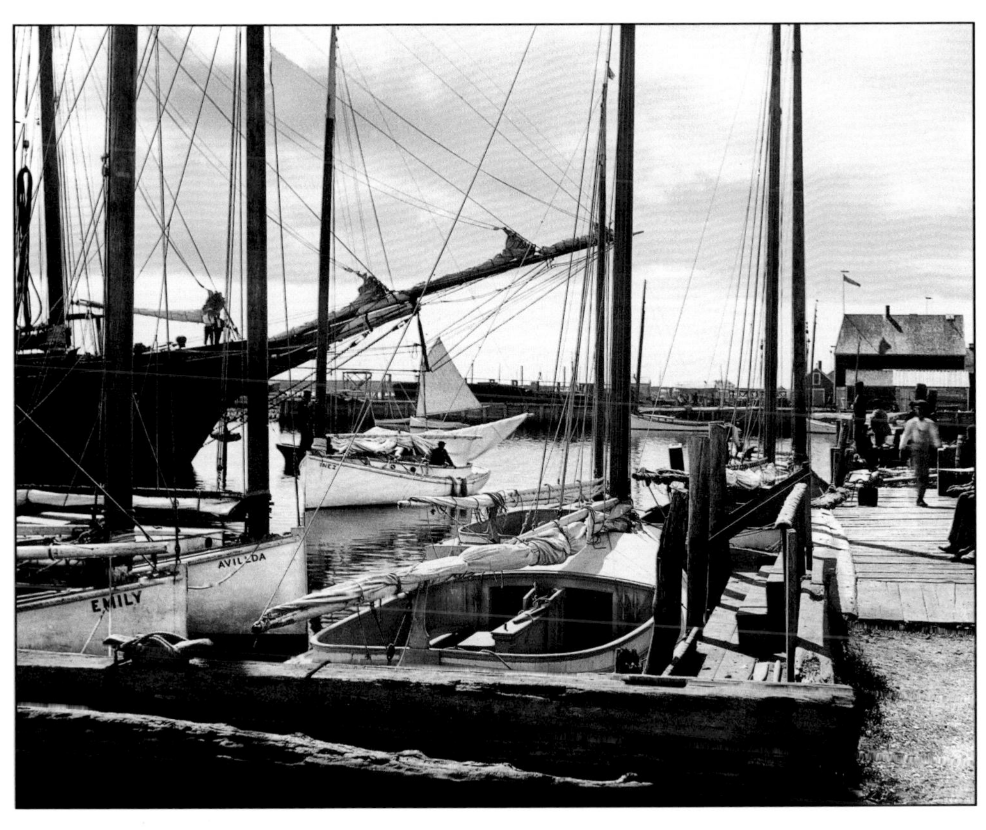

Plate 34

Accession Number: 1983.70.66 *EMILY, AVILLDA, INEZ* docked with schooner *MINNIE(?)* in background. Glass plate negative.

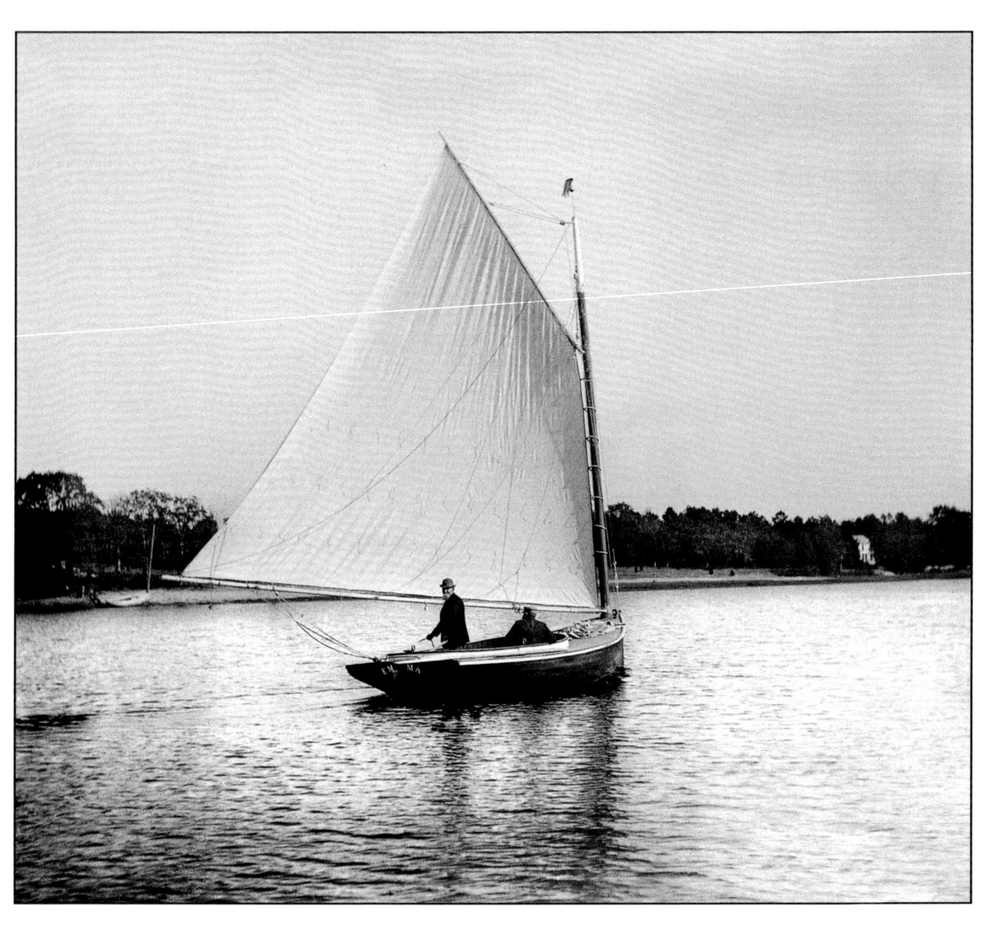

Plate 35

Accession Number: 1984.185.1 *EMMA.* Dry plate negative.

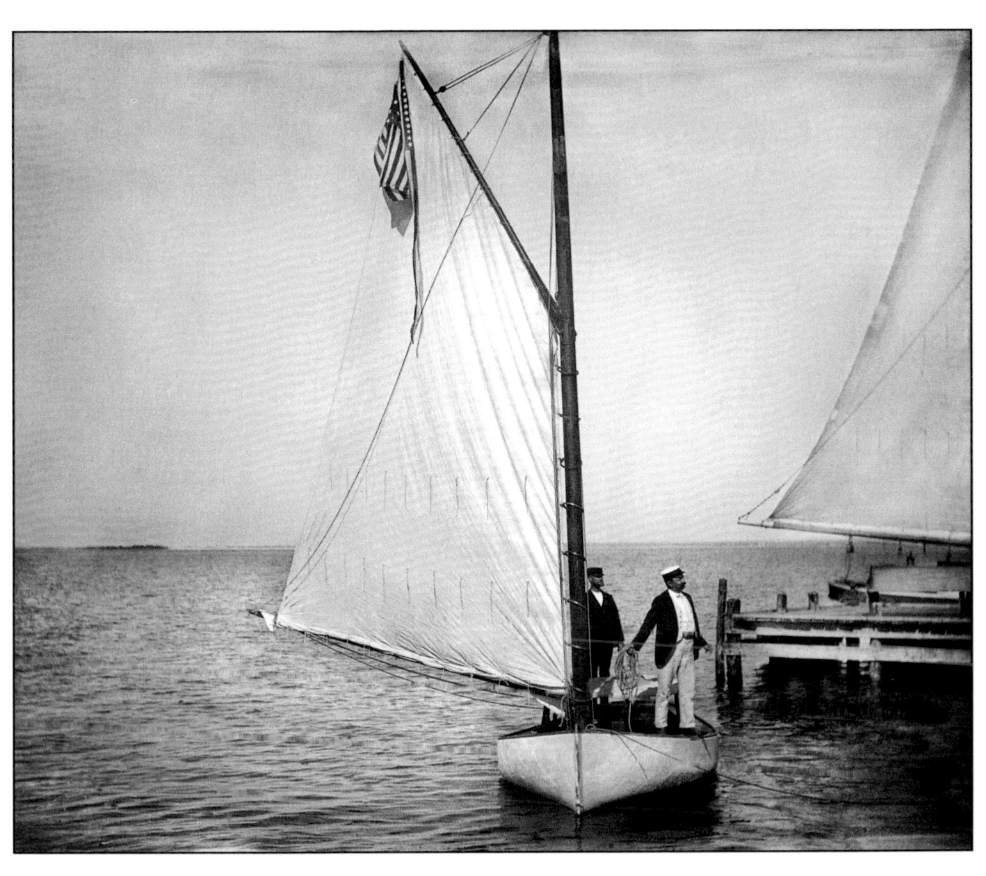

Plate 36

Accession Number: 1984.185.4 *UNIDENTIFIED* vessel. Dry plate negative.

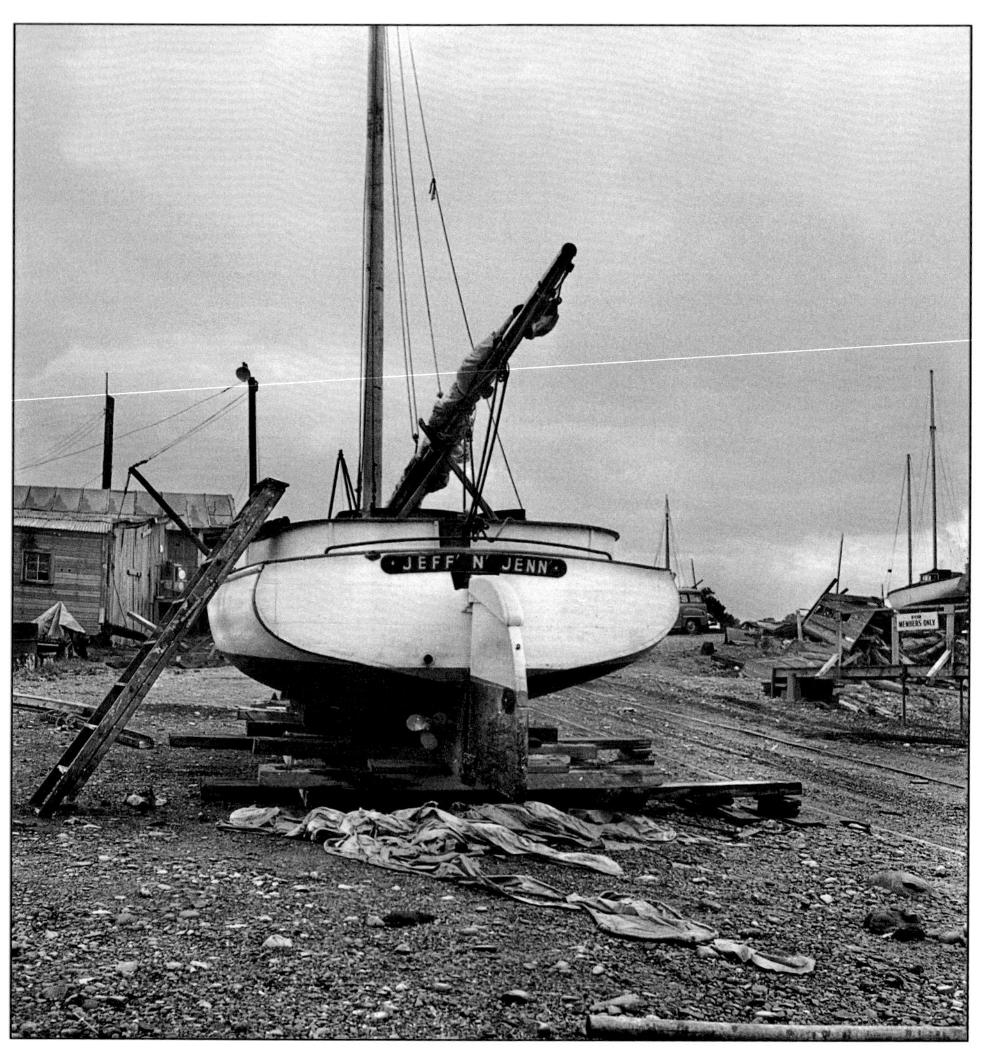

Plate 37

Accession Number: 1986.16.755 *JEFF N' JENN* hauled for maintanence.

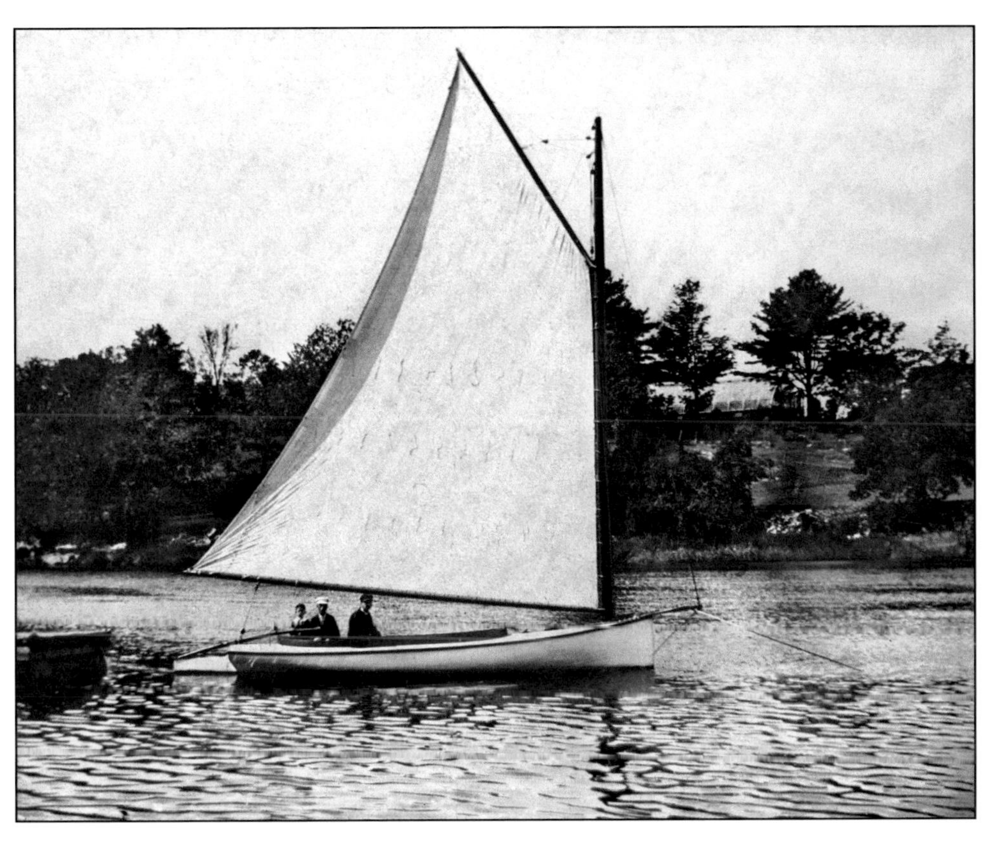

Plate 38

Accession Number: 1980.57.1 *CRITIC* at anchor.

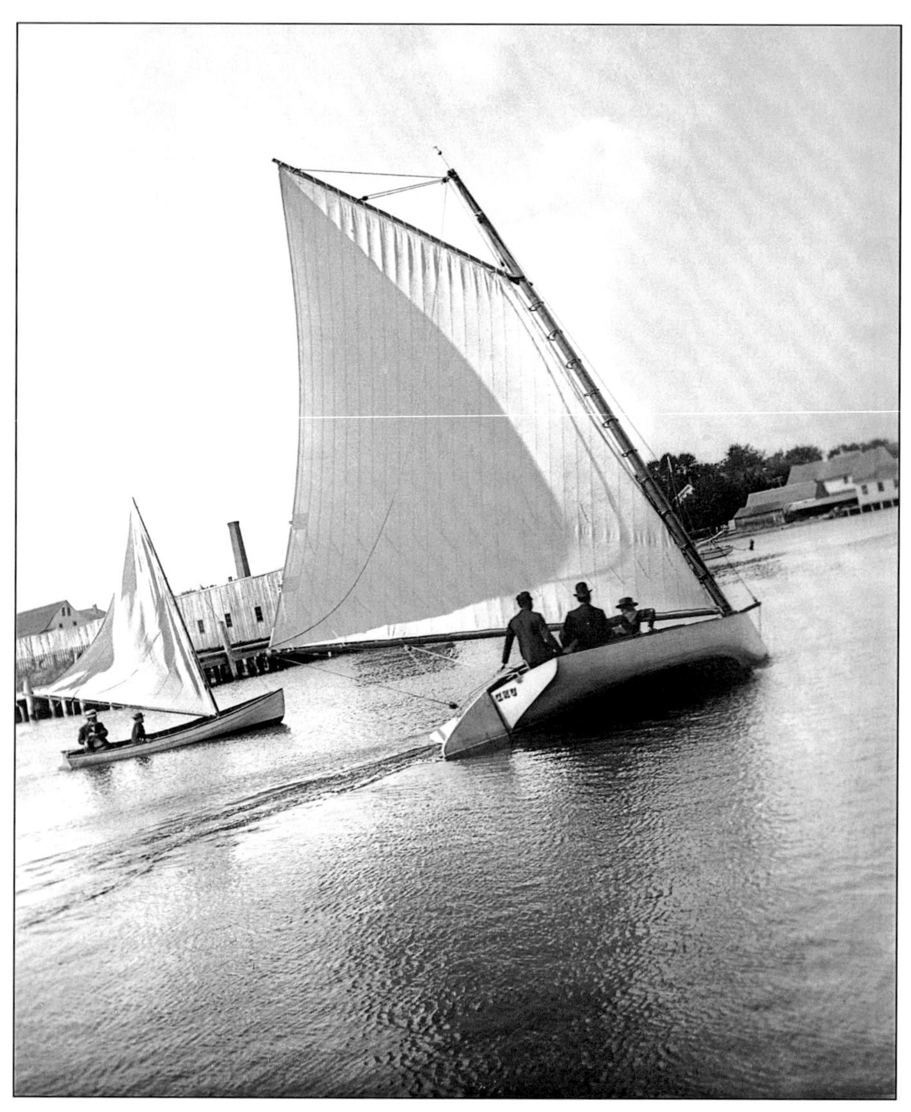

Plate 39

Accession Number: 1977.92.471 *UNDINE* sailing on the Mystic River, CT. Photograph by E.A. Scholfield. Gelatin glass plate negative.

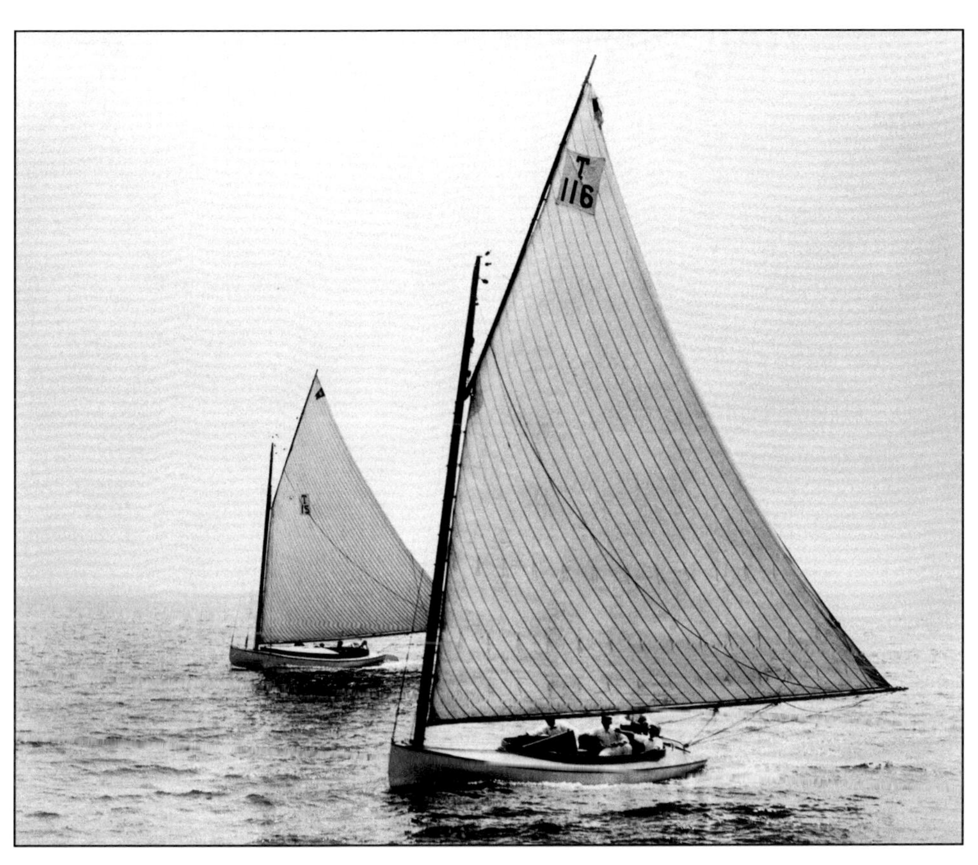

Plate 40

Accession Number: 1993.17.212 *EDWINA* and *UNIDENTIFIED* vessel.

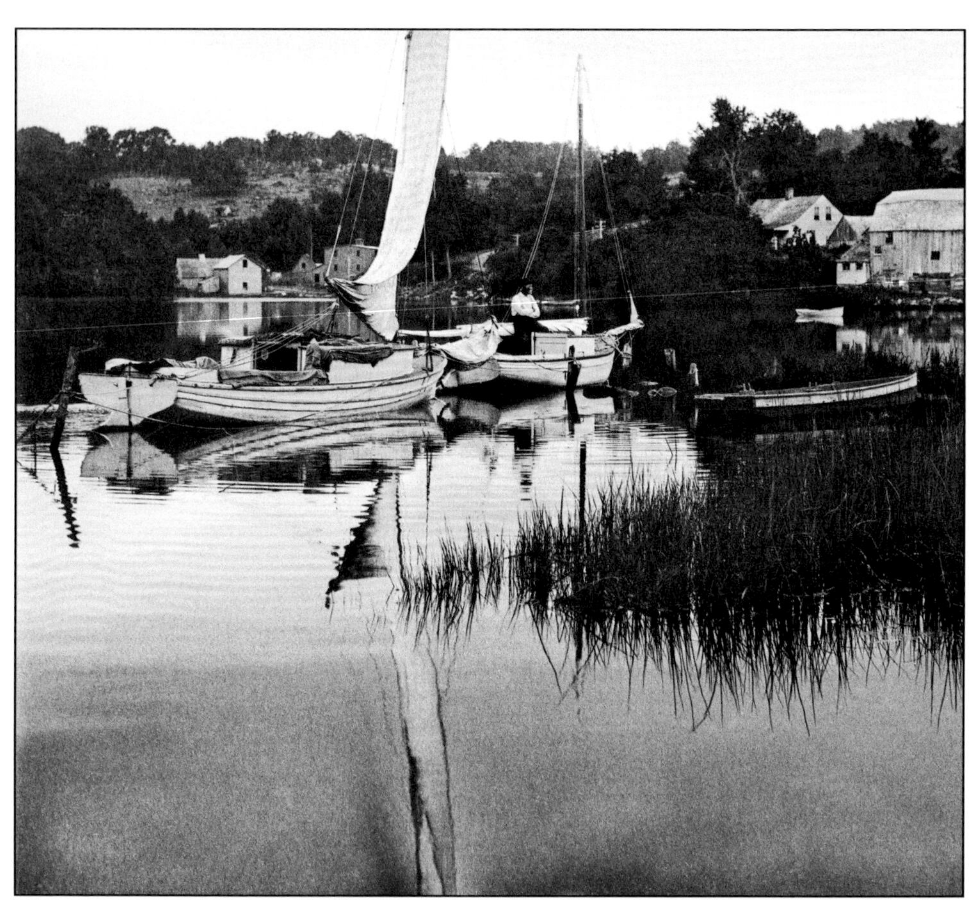

Plate 41

Accession Number: 1993.17.406 *UNIDENTIFIED* vessels on the Mystic River, CT. Photograph by George E. Tingley.

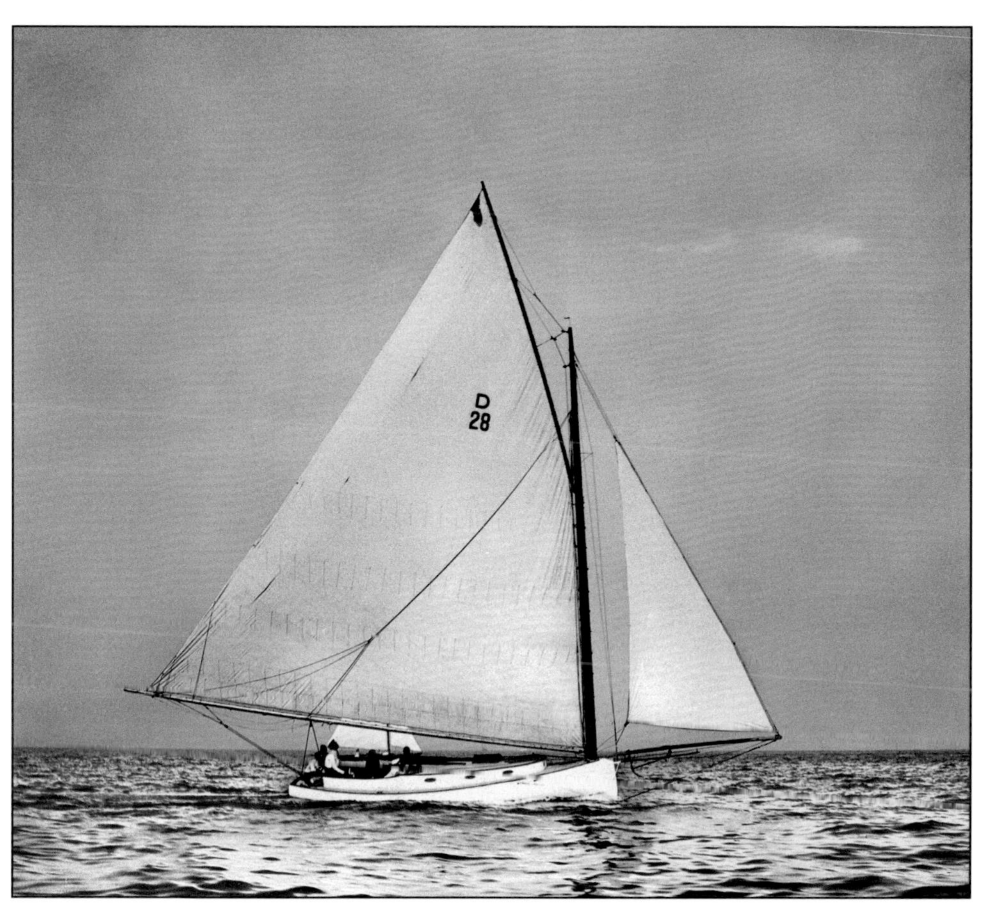

Plate 42

Accession Number: 1990.37.847 *DARTWELL*

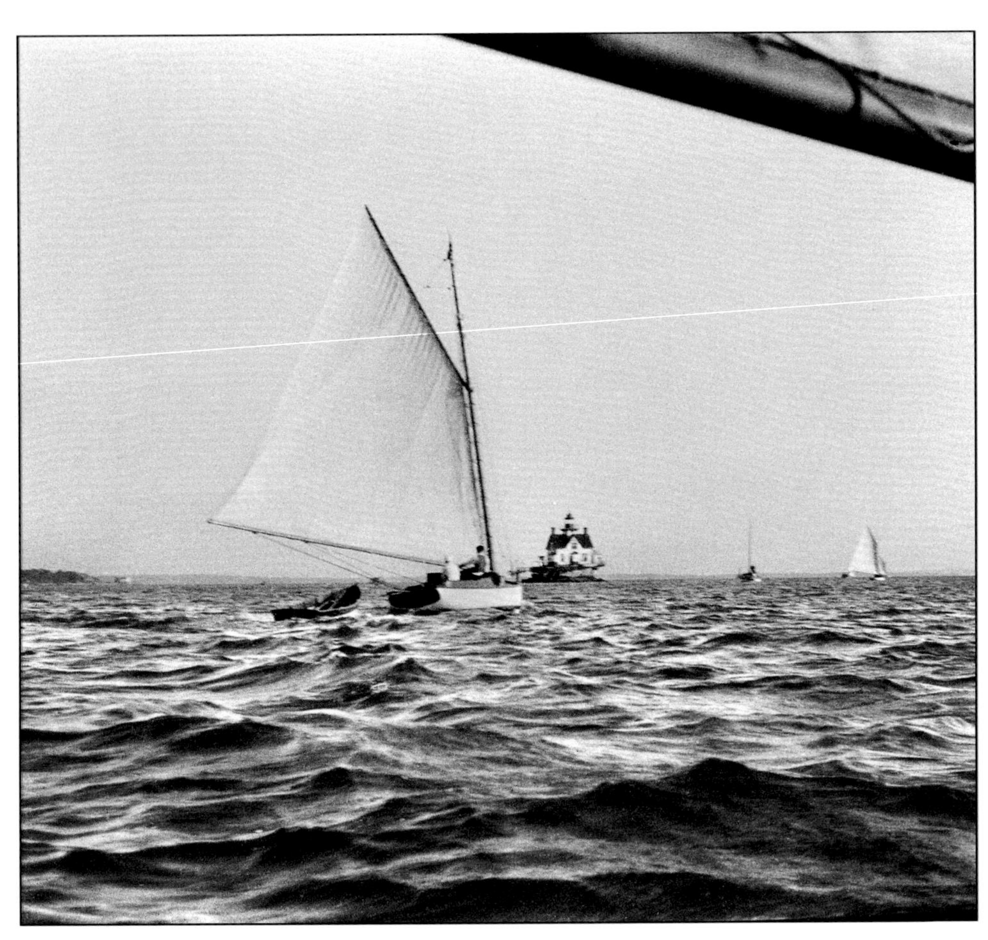

Plate 43

Accession Number: 1990.67.73 *UNIDENTIFIED* vessel probably sailing in Rhode Island waters. Photograph from Budlong family album.

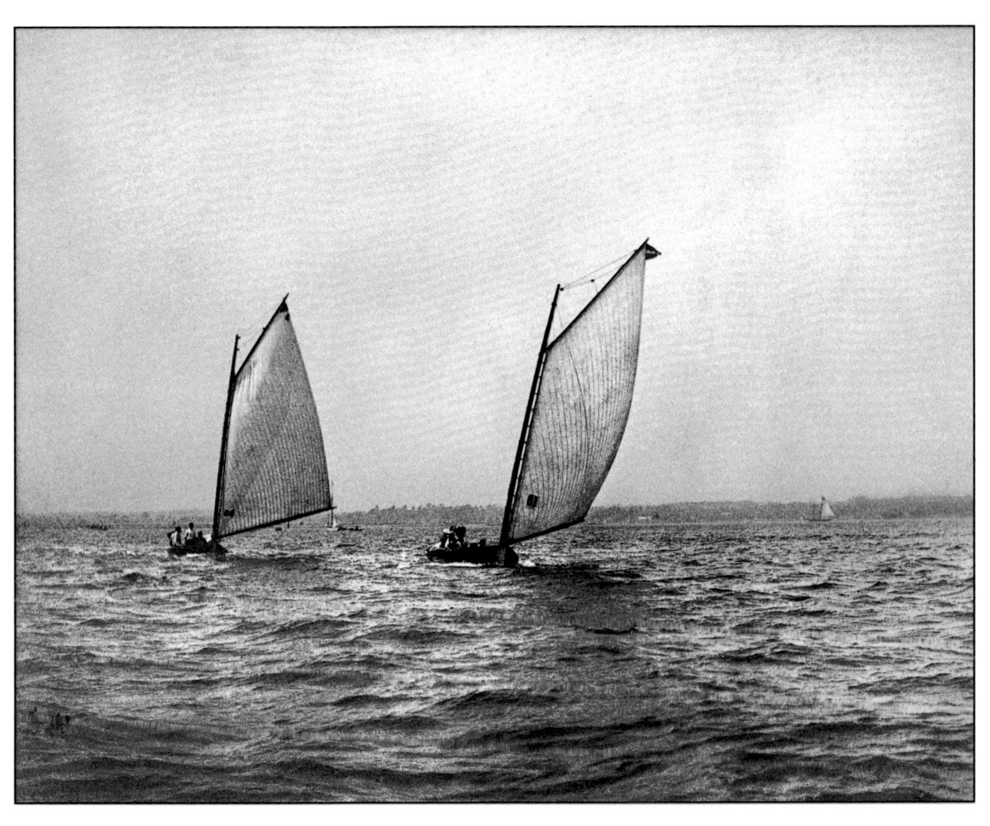

Plate 44

Accession Number: 1995.20.2 *UNIDENTIFIED* vessels from Cedar Point Yacht Club, ca. 1890. Albumen print.

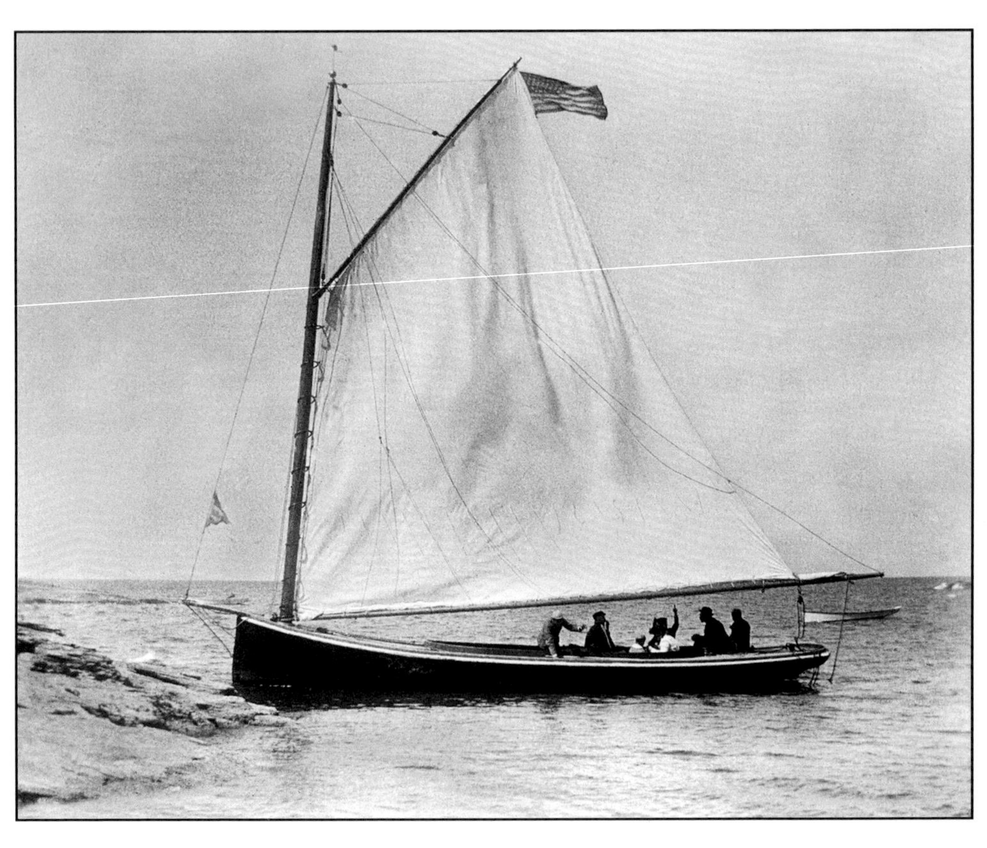

Plate 45

Accession Number: 1974.4.110 *CAPTAIN'S BOAT* Crescent Bluff, Niantic, CT
Glass plate negative.

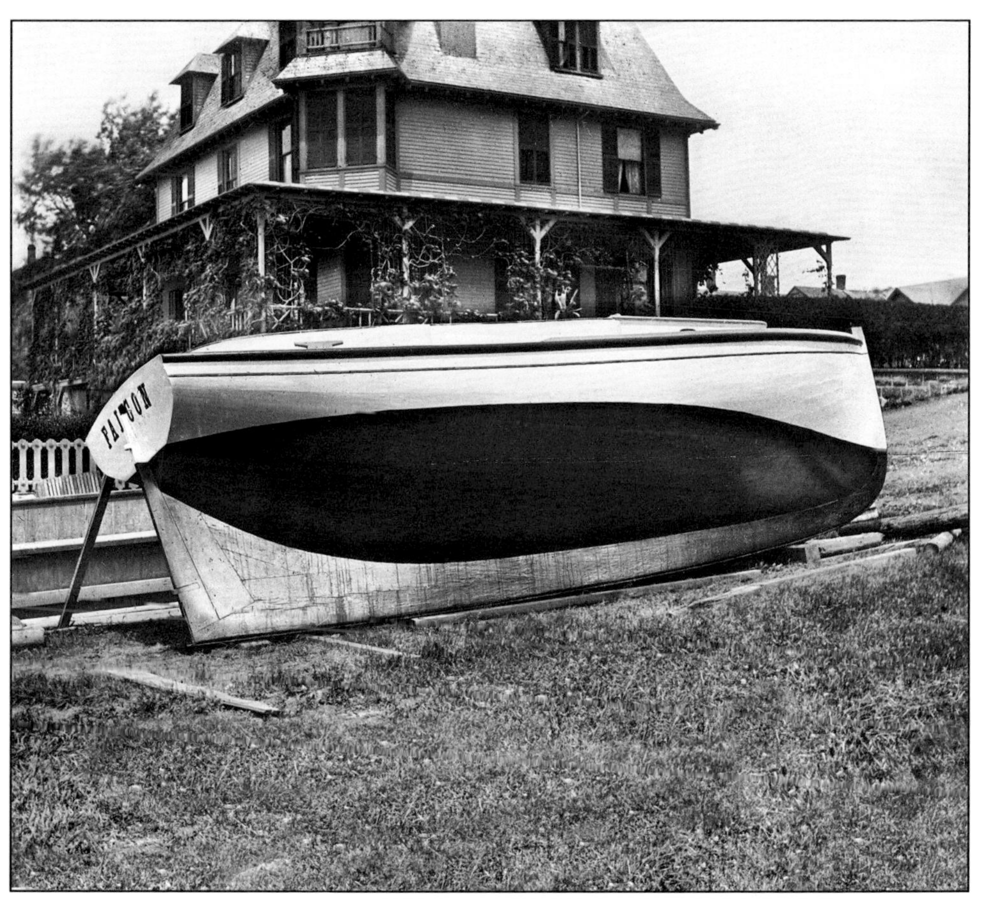

Plate 46

Accession Number: 1981.159.17 *FALCON.* Designed by Z. Hallett, Built by H.L. Lambert, Hyannis, Ma 1889. Photo by Edward W. Smith, ca. 1890-1905. Gelatin Glass Plate. Vessel size: 25’ x 11’ 9” x 3’

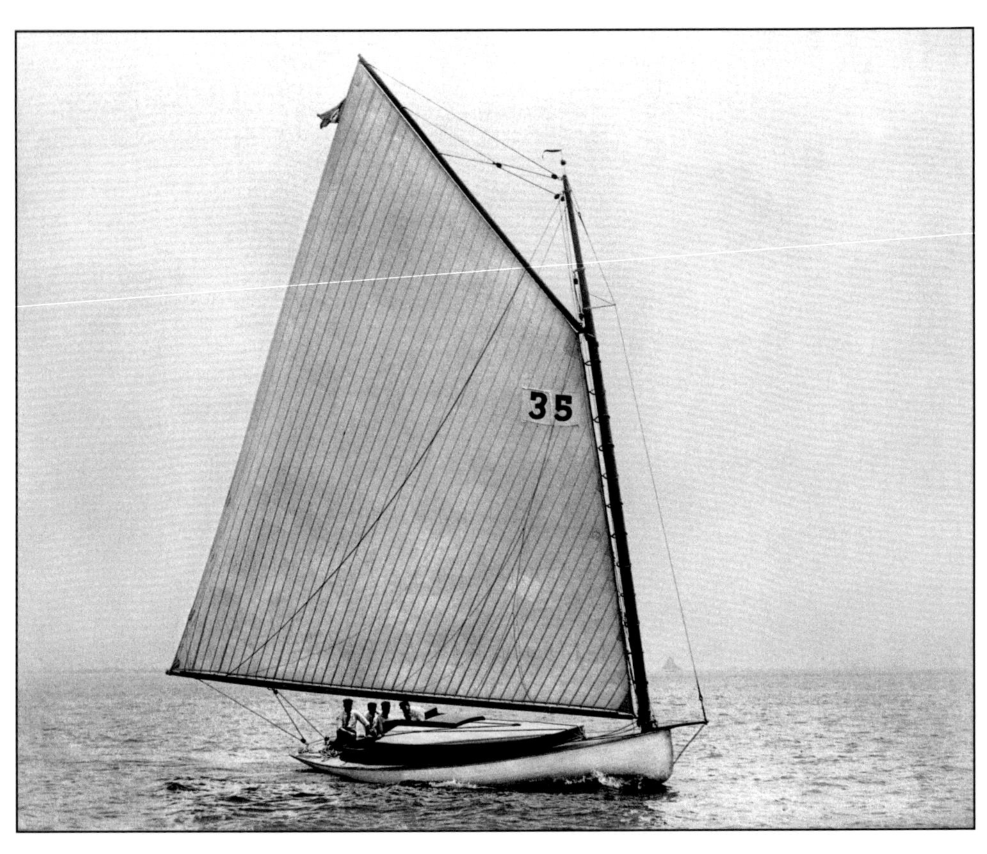

Plate 47

Accession Number: 1993.17.204 *OCONEE*

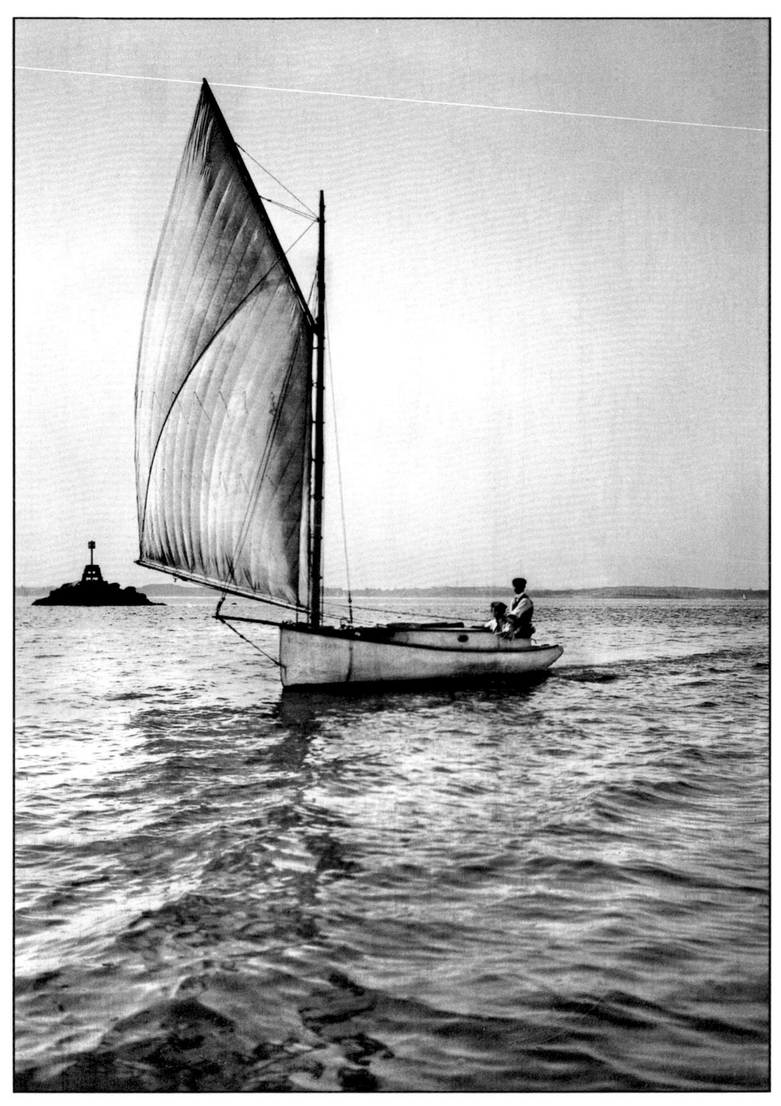

Plate 48

Accession Number: 1976.208.336 *UNIDENTIFIED* vessel.

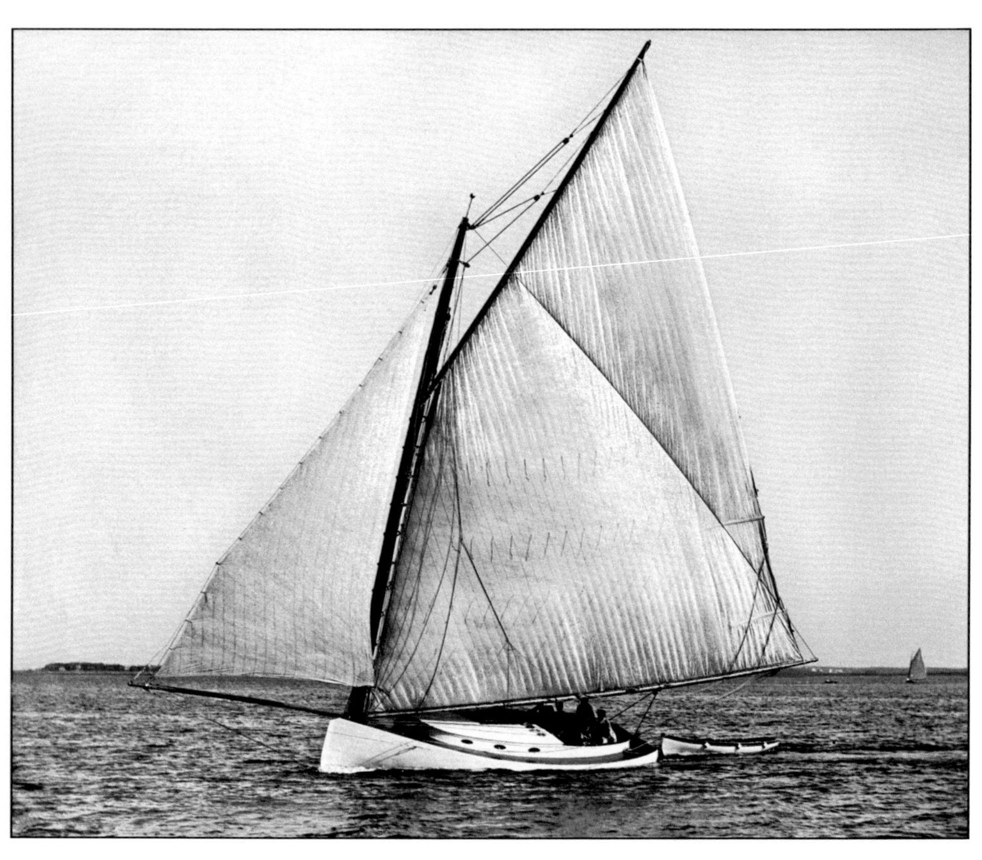

Plate 49

Accession Number: 1993.17.213 *HARBINGER*

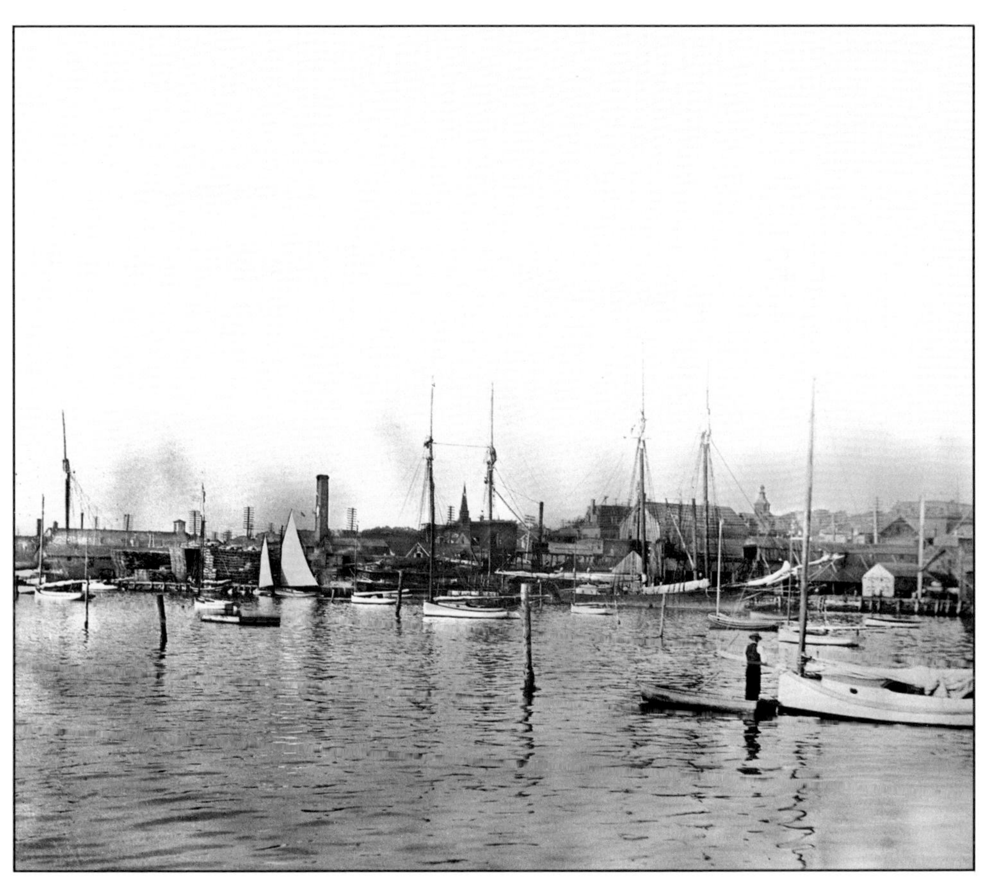

Plate 50

Accession Number: 1982.84.71 *UNIDENTIFIED* vessels in harbor. Boatbuilder Lars Larsen in skiff at bow of catboat.

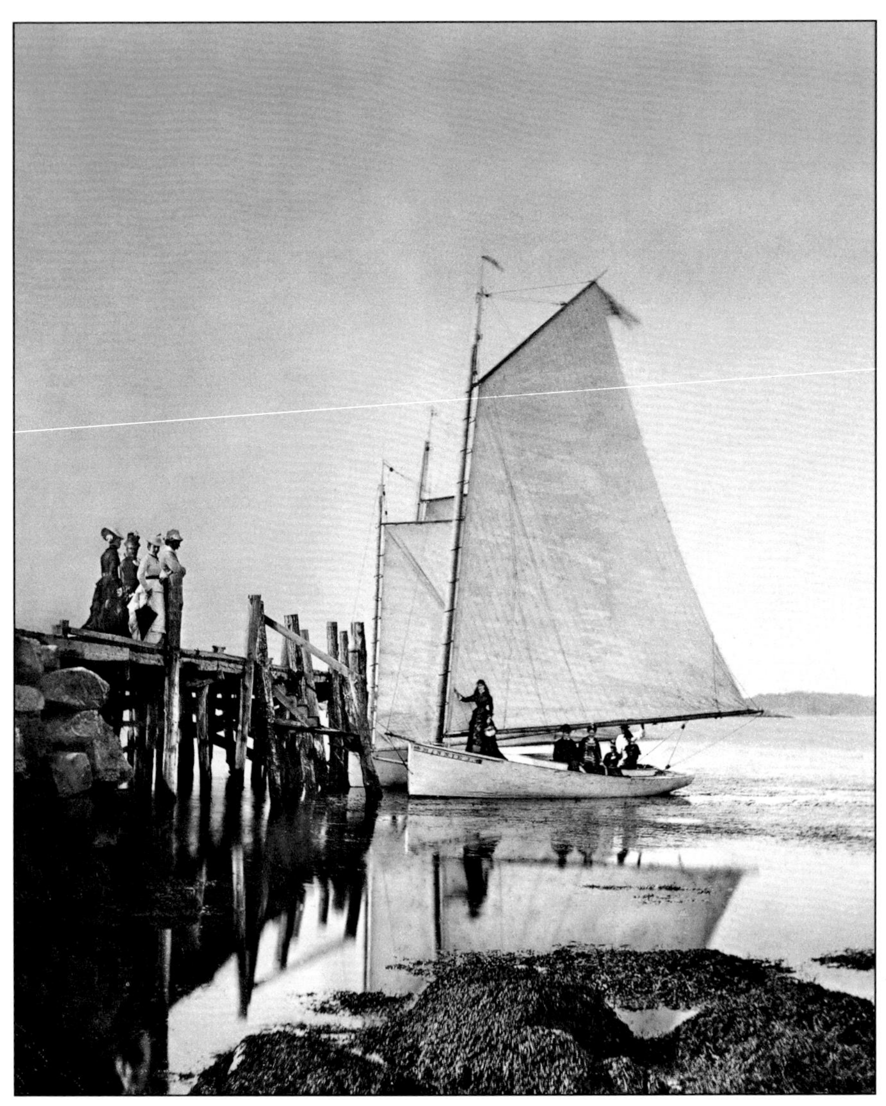

Plate 51

Accession Number: 1977.92.366 *MINNIE J* possibly at Mystic Island at mouth of Mystic River, CT. Photograph by E.A. Scholfield. Collodion glass plate negative.

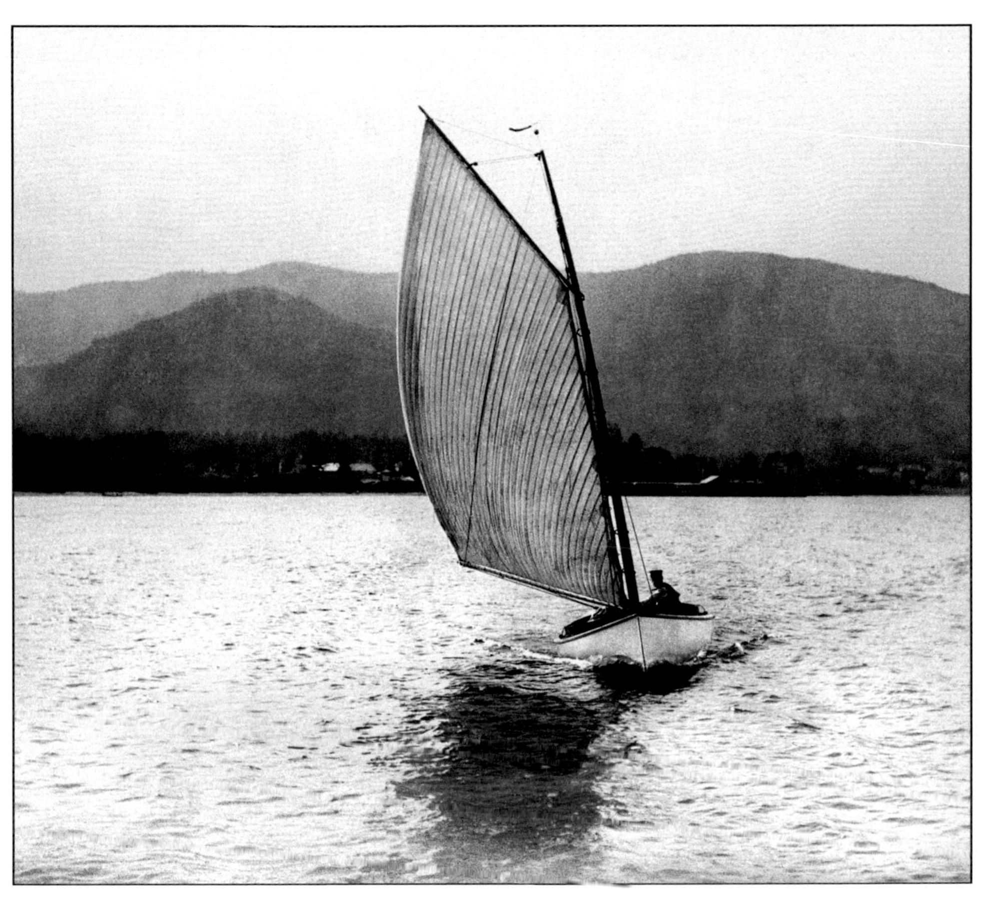

Plate 52

Accession Number: 1993.6.6 *MARY*

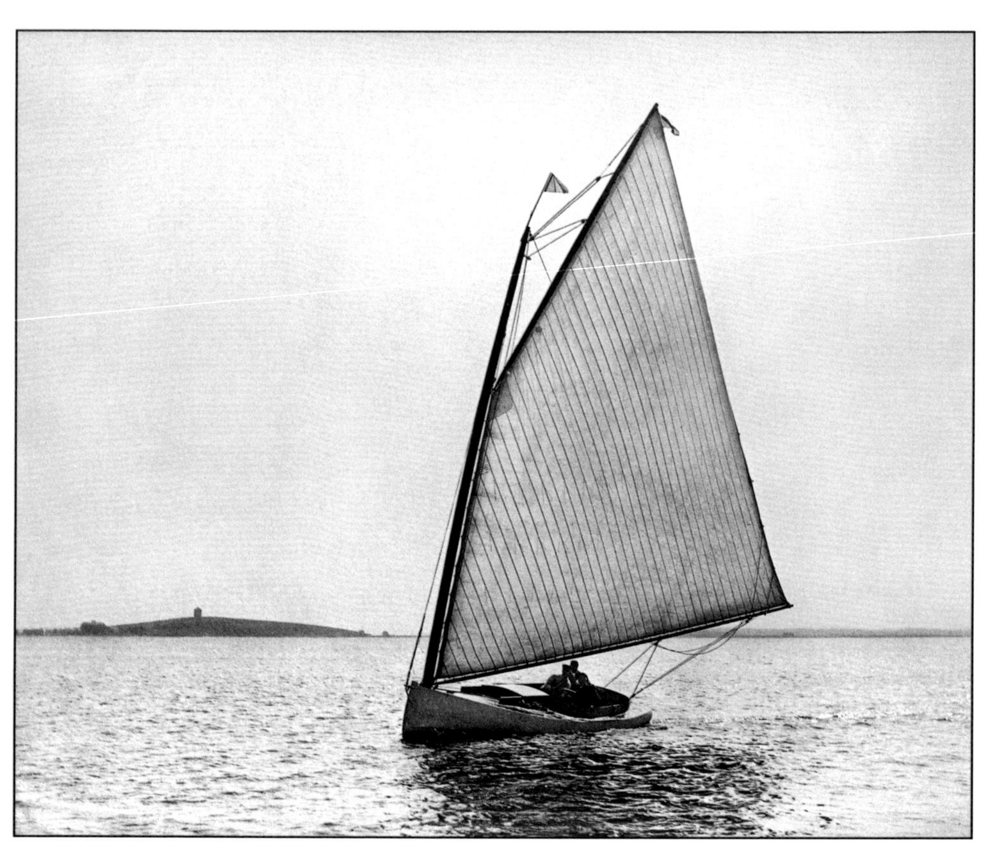

Plate 53

Accession Number: 1993.17.271 *EGERIA*

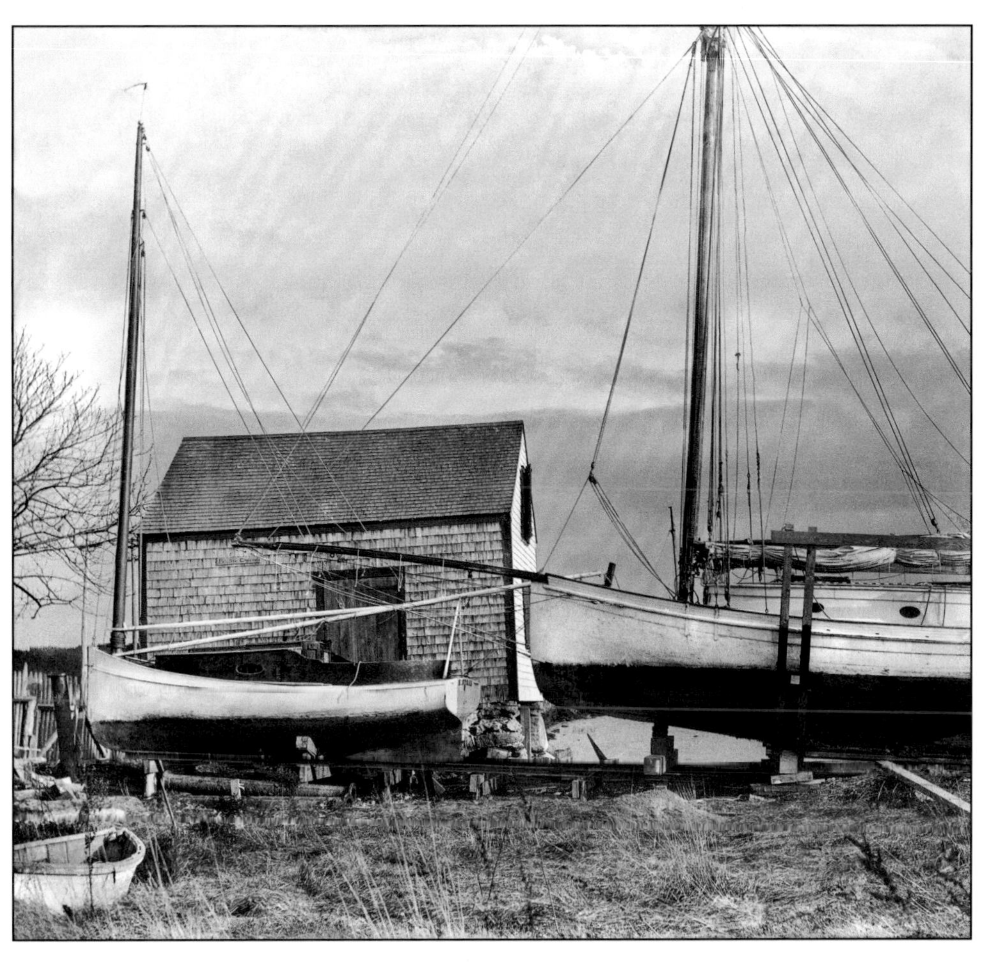

Plate 54

Accession Number: 1985.1.4 *MISTRAL* and *UNIDENTIFIED* catboat.
Gelatin dryplate negative.

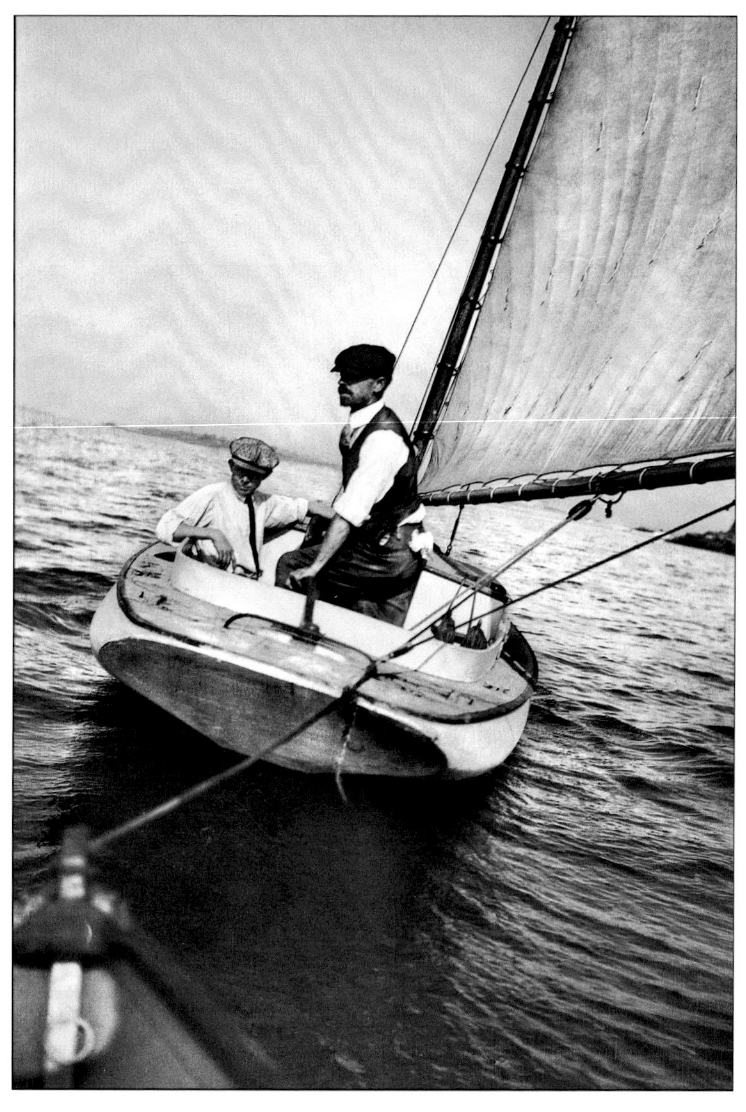

Plate 55

Accession Number: 1976.208.334 *UNIDENTIFIED* vessel towing tender.

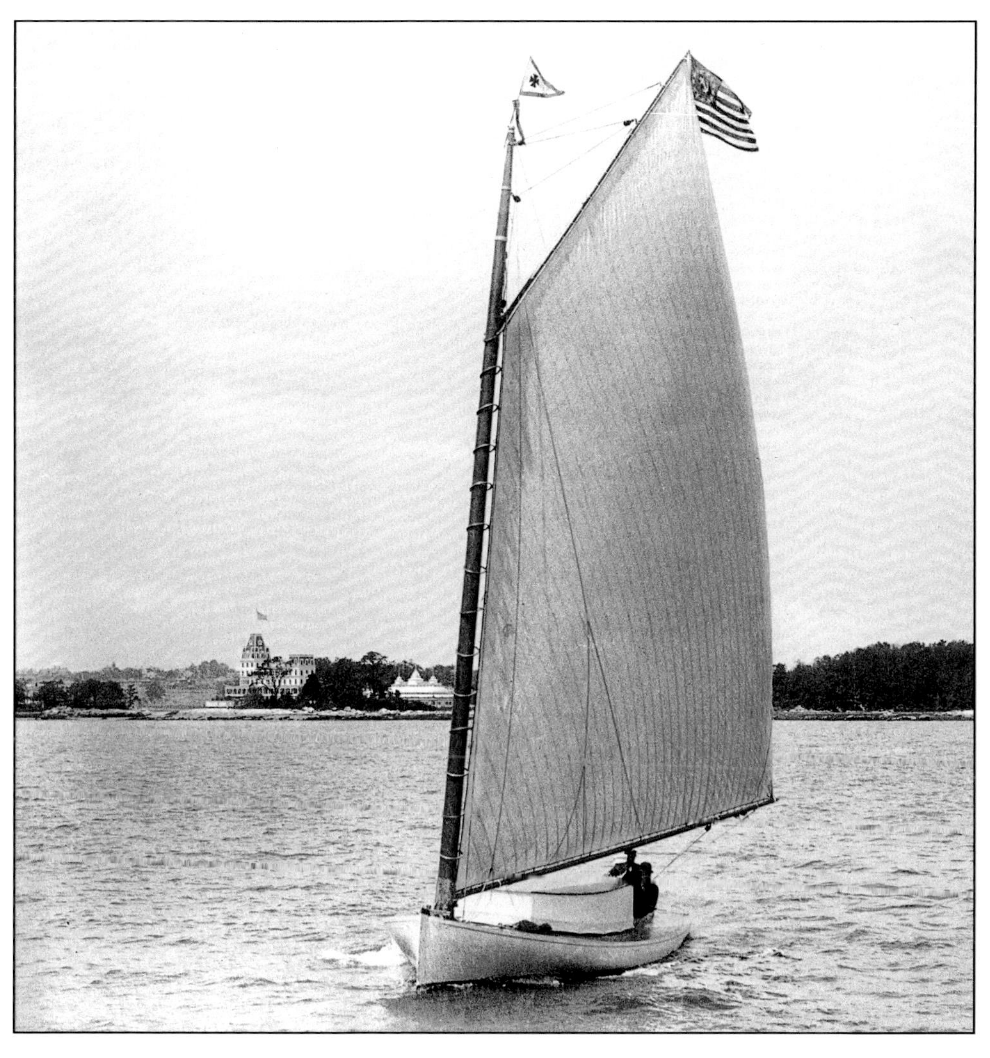

Plate 56

Accession Number: 1985.82.13 *DOT* Flying the Riverside Yacht Club Burgee.
Stereograph Album Print.

Footnotes

The introductory information came from the two books listed below.
For a complete picture of the origins of the catboat and its evolution see:

[1] Chapelle, Howard I., *American Small Sailing Craft*, NY, Norton & Co. 1951

Leavens, John, M., *The Catboat Book*, Middleboro, MA, The Catboat Association with International Marine, 1973

[2] Alden, William L., *The Flying Proa*, NY, Harper's New Monthly Magazine, 1878

Other Books by Markham Starr

Building a Greenland Kayak

Against the Tide: The Commercial Fishermen of Point Judith

On Oceans of Grey: Portrait of a Fishing Port